Costume

Costume

JAMES LAVER

HAWTHORN BOOKS, INC.
PUBLISHERS
NEW YORK

First American Edition, March 1964

Printed in Great Britain
H–2902

Contents

Ashur-nasir-pal II, King of Assyria, 883–859 B.C. *From a statue in the British Museum.*

CHAPTER ONE

Primitive Times and Early Civilizations

Man is unique among the animals in wearing clothes, and the question arises as to why he should do so. Until a generation or so ago it was widely believed that there was an obvious answer. According to the Book of Genesis, Adam and Eve 'knew that they were naked' when they had eaten of the fruit of the tree of the knowledge of good and evil. They therefore made themselves 'aprons' of fig-leaves.

Belief in the literal truth of the Garden of Eden story in the Bible is not widely held nowadays, but many people still think that men and women wear clothes because they have an innate feeling of modesty. Anthropologists (that is, those scientists who have made a special study of the history of Man) point out, however, that modesty varies from age to age and from place to place. An Arab woman still considers it immodest to uncover her face; a Chinese lady of fifty years ago thought it immodest to show her feet; to a prudish Victorian lady it was quite unthinkable to reveal the legs. Modesty, in short, turns out to be a matter of convention, and as the great anthropologist, Westermarck, remarks: 'The facts appear to prove that the feeling of shame, far from being the cause of man's covering his body, is, on the contrary, a result of this custom.' Men and women never 'knew that they were naked' until the wearing of clothes had become so habitual that taking them off in public had something surprising and shocking about it.

Another obvious theory which turns out, on examination, to be unfounded is that people began to wear clothes because they were cold. Once again anthropologists disagree with this idea, and are able to cite numerous examples of primitive tribes who go about naked in spite of the rigours of the climate. Tierra del Fuego, in South America, is a cold region, but the inhabitants have never taken what seems to us the obvious step of inventing clothes. Instead, they suspend from their necks a kind of shield of hide which they shift

1

about according to the direction of the wind. On the other hand, the bedouin of Arabia wear a considerable quantity of clothing in spite of the intense heat.

But if neither modesty nor protection against the weather is the explanation of wearing clothes, why have clothes ever been worn at all? The scientific answer is so remote from our modern notions that we have to make some effort of the imagination to understand it at all. It does seem, from the evidence available, that clothes had originally a 'magical' origin. Primitive men and women were dominated by fear of spirits and of witchcraft, in particular that form of malevolent magic known as the 'evil eye'. They were afraid that a mere look from an evilly disposed person might strike them with disease or weakness and they tried to protect themselves against this danger by wearing amulets or, as we would say, lucky charms.

From times long before the period of recorded history, the belief in amulets was universal, and the most popular amulet was the cowrie shell. This was supposed to give special protection against childlessness—in primitive times thought to be the most dreadful misfortune that could happen to anyone. Girdles and aprons of cowrie shells are found to have been used all over the world, even in places far from the sea, and such shells were so highly prized that they were actually used as money.

Amulets were attached to the body by cords at places where they could not easily slip off: at waist, neck, wrists and ankles. The waist cord was the most important, and objects suspended from it were generally hung in front where they could be most clearly seen. From the waist cord also could be hung some kind of pouch or purse, of which the most modern relic is the Scotsman's sporran—only primitive man wore, so to speak, the sporran without the kilt.

And now another element enters into the development of clothing and we can call this vanity, or display. It is obvious that the woman with the most cowrie shells tied round her waist would be the wife of the most successful warrior or chief, and so these decorations began to have a social meaning. The warrior liked to adorn his body with the teeth of wild beasts killed in the chase. These too were thought to have a magical quality for the strength of the animal was supposed to be contained in them. They were also trophies and indicated that the wearer of such teeth, in the form, for example, of a necklace, was a mighty hunter. They increased his self-confidence and indicated his importance to others. Even such a simple action as sticking a feather in the hair enhanced the pride of life, for it was not just anyone who would dare to do this. If a man stuck too many feathers in his hair, he was likely to provoke the jealousy of the other men of the tribe. He had to fight for the right to wear his feathers and, very soon, only the most successful fighters were allowed to have feathers in any number. This tradition can be seen to this day among American Indians where the Big Chief wears a whole crown of feathers and the ordinary braves but one. The strongest and most important man is the most gorgeously decorated and in this we can see the origin of class distinction in dress. The wearing of clothes by women led to an even more interesting development, for it was found that clothes could be made attractive to the opposite sex, and in this we can see the origin of fashion.

Much has been discovered in recent years concerning the early history of man and of his remote ancestors. Of the most remote it is difficult to say whether they were really

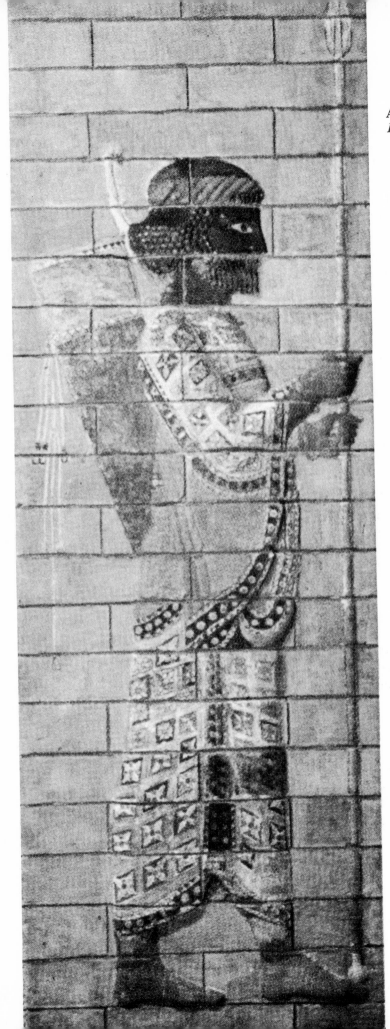

Archer. *Glazed tile from the Palace of Darius at Susa, now in the British Museum.*

3

men or not. The anthropologists have decided that the dividing line is determined by the use of tools. However ape-like in appearance some of our earlier ancestors may have been, if they used tools, even of the most primitive form, they are classified as men. Some authorities believe that Heidelberg Man (called after the fragmentary remains which were discovered in Heidelberg) may have used his powerful jaws for chewing the skins of animals to make them pliable enough for clothing. The Eskimos do so to this day, thus keeping up a practice which has been in operation for something like two hundred thousand years. Yet teeth are hardly tools in the accepted sense. Neanderthal Man, who came much later, and was a cave-dweller, certainly had tools, some of them very similar in form to those still used by tanners. It is thought that the women dressed the skins while the men went hunting; but they had not reached the stage of being able to sew the skins into a garment.

A superior race called Cromagnon (once again after the place where remains have been found) replaced the Neanderthal during what is known as the Upper Palæolithic Period. Palæolithic means 'old stone' and refers to the fact that men at this time made their tools by chipping pieces of flint to obtain a point and a cutting edge. They even managed to make bone needles with pierced eyes and only a little larger than modern ones. It is safe to assume therefore that they sewed skins together to make clothes, and in a cave in Spain there is a mural painting showing people wearing skin garments somewhat resembling those of the modern Eskimo. In a similar cave in France have been found toggles or double-buttons, and even a hairpin in such a position near a skeleton as to leave no doubt about its use.

COSTUME

Hilaire Hiler, one of the greatest authorities on primitive costume, tells us that most of the chief forms of European dress (remaining unchanged in essentials until the middle of the fourteenth century A.D.) were already established in this period, probably including, 'a simple tunic, the ancestor of a long line of similar pieces, the skirt or kilt [or divided coverings for the legs], the mantle or cape [precursor of the coat] as well as moccasins or boots'.

Skirts and divided coverings for the legs (that is, trousers) seem to us to be essentially different garments, but the distinction lay, originally, merely in the way in which hide (or, later, cloth) was worn. If it hung free from the hips it was the forerunner of the skirt; if any portion of it was passed between the legs it was the ancestor of trousers. We think of men as wearing trousers and women as wearing skirts, but this rule has had so many exceptions that a different distinction has been proposed, between arctic and tropical clothes, people in cold climates wearing trousers and people in hot climates wearing skirts. We must, however, consider this matter later when we come to the costume of the Greeks and Romans.

The Palæolithic (or 'old stone') Age was succeeded by the Neolithic (or 'new stone') Age, which lasted in Europe from about twenty thousand to six thousand years ago. Man was now capable of making more efficient tools although they were still of stone, and also of making cloth. It was found that strands of animal or vegetable fibre (wool or flax) could be made into thread by twisting. This was first done by hand and then by a primitive form of spindle. The threads so obtained were then plaited together and later woven by means

4

of a simple loom. Fragments of both plaited and woven cloth of the Neolithic Period have been found in Switzerland and elsewhere.

The next step was to dye the cloth in different colours, the favourites being red, yellow and blue. It is probable that these earth and vegetable colours were the only ones obtainable, and they were not very bright. Primitive man seems to have been particularly fond of red, not only for its obvious attractiveness (very young children are said to be able to distinguish red before they become conscious of other colours) but also because it was the colour of blood. Blood was associated with life and so the colour red was thought to be endowed with magical properties. The lavish use of red pigment in prehistoric burials is thought to have indicated a desire, if not to restore the corpse to life, at least to give it strength for its passing into the next world.

A good deal is known about the costume of the ancient Egyptians. A multitude of wall paintings, statues, ornaments and even clothes are preserved in tombs; all these enable us to paint a picture of Egyptian life which is probably more complete than is possible for any other ancient civilization. From 3000 B.C. onwards the records are gradually more extensive, and perhaps the most surprising thing about Egyptian costume is the comparatively small amount of change to be noted.

At the beginning of this long period, the Egyptians of what is called the Old Kingdom wore a loin-cloth of woven material wrapped round the body and secured by a belt. This garment was known as a *schenti*. Important persons wore it pleated and stiffened into a kind of triangular apron which for the Pharaohs was sometimes richly embroidered. It is thought that the stiff radiating pleats represented the rays of the sun. Under the New Kingdom (1500 B.C. to 332 B.C.) the Pharaohs wore, in addition, a long fringed tunic called *kalasiris* and above it a kind of ample cloak made of almost transparent linen gauze. The *kalasiris* was itself semi-transparent so that the loin-cloth underneath it could still be seen.

Scholars distinguish between various types of *kalasiris*: some with sleeves and some without; and they could be wide or narrow—sometimes so narrow as to make movement of the limbs almost impossible. In its simplest form the garment consisted of a rectangular piece of material. A round hole was cut in the middle through which the head was inserted. The sides were then sewn together leaving space for the armholes. When sleeves were required these were, in general, cut separately and sewn on. Sometimes, however, the *kalasiris* was woven or knitted in one piece. The former type resembled a woman's petticoat; the latter was a sheath-like garment which, when worn by women, often finished below the breasts and was kept in place either by a high girdle or by shoulder straps.

Another garment worn by both men and women was the cape, generally just long enough to cover the shoulders. In its earliest form it was almost circular, either with a hole for the head in the middle or made to fasten at the back. Later it was rectangular in form. Both sexes wore the characteristic wide collar of beads or jewels. There was a lavish display of bracelets and armlets. In early times only the priests wore sandals, but later they were worn by all important personages. They consisted of soles made of leather, papyrus or wood, kept in place by straps.

One of the most striking items of Egyptian costume throughout its history was the wig. The Nile Valley can be extremely hot and, very early, Egyptian men and women began

5

6   **The Lady Ninofretmin.** *Egyptian statuette, c. 2600 B.C., in the British Museum.*

to shave their heads and, for ceremonial occasions, to wear artificial hair, of such hair-like materials as flax, wool or palm-fibre. The poorer people wore wigs of felt. Wigs have been found in early tombs of the Old Kingdom and the custom of wearing them lasted for thousands of years. Hats were not worn, but the Pharaohs had a symbolic head-gear rather like a helmet or mitre. The war helmet was made of metal and adorned with two ostrich feathers. After the conquest of Alexander the Great there was some modification in the direction of Greek modes, but, in the main, the Egyptians retained their characteristic costume until the time of the Romans.

The early civilizations arose in the fertile river valleys, and what the Nile was to the Egyptians, the Euphrates and the Tigris were to the people of Mesopotamia. A high degree of culture had been established around Babylon in Sumerian days (3000 B.C. to 2000 B.C.), but by the later date the Babylonian Empire had been replaced by the Assyrian which reached its culmination about 1300 B.C. The combined culture which resulted dominated the Middle East for many centuries.

The characteristic costume consisted of a shirt with short, tight sleeves, worn either with or without a belt. Slaves and the lower classes generally (and also priests, of whom considerable activity was demanded during sacrificial ceremonies) wore it knee length, but for kings and nobles it reached to the ankles. Important personages had a tasselled girdle and over the shirt or tunic wore a kind of shoulder-cape which was either fastened on one shoulder with a clasp—the other end being drawn forward under the arm—or made with holes through which the head and one arm could be inserted.

The cloak, and the undergarment too, gradually became more elaborate, being patterned or embroidered and edged with fringes. The garments were brightly coloured but purple and gold were reserved for the king. An additional garment for the king and members of his court was a long stole or shoulder-scarf of rich material and elaborately fringed. Degrees of rank were indicated by the manner in which the scarf was worn and its design; the prime minister, or grand vizier, for example, wore his crossed over the breast, and minor officials had shorter fringes. The high priest, and the king himself when he officiated in this capacity, wore above his other garments a cloak of peculiar shape, cut all in one piece, and, once more, heavily fringed. Fringes, indeed, are the characteristic mark of Babylonian and Assyrian costume.

Primitive Times and Early Civilizations

Both men and women wore their hair long; the men grew theirs into a kind of chignon at the back, two plaits being crossed beneath it and their ends brought up and fastened over the forehead. Hair and beards were elaborately curled and sometimes interwoven with gold thread. The characteristic head-dress was in the form of a terraced and truncated cone, rather like an inverted flowerpot. Ear-rings and bracelets were worn by all high officials and rich men.

Comparatively little is known of women's dress, as they are seldom represented in the bas-reliefs discovered at Nineveh. Goddesses are shown in long flounced robes, but it is probable that high ranking women wore embroidered and fringed garments very similar to those of the men. Their hair, also, was dressed in a chignon of a rather more elaborate form. Both sexes went barefoot, except for warriors who wore a high laced boot or buskin.

In the sixth century B.C. the Babylonian civilization was overrun by the Persians.

King Mery-ānkh-Rā. *Egyptian statuette, c. 1400* B.C., *in the British Museum.*

These hardy warriors from the mountains of what is now called Turkestan, who had been accustomed to clothe themselves in the skins of wild beasts, soon adopted the costumes of the more cultured people they had conquered: the long fringed tunic and the over-garments which have been described. These clothes, however, fitted the body more closely and were made not only of wool and linen but sometimes of silk, it being by this time possible to obtain this precious material by caravan from China. A striking innovation was the wearing of trousers, and it would seem, from the very scanty records available, that these were also worn by women. The characteristic footgear was a shoe, or ankle-boot, of supple leather.

The hair was bushy and almost shoulder-length. Important personages curled their beards like the Assyrians. The head-dress, however, was quite different. The early Persian head-dress was a kind of soft, felt cap which the Greeks knew as the Phrygian cap, and which was revived at the French Revolution as the 'red cap of Liberty'. Another form was a kind of low crowned toque, sometimes curving out at the top in the form still used by the clergy of the Greek Orthodox Church.

The Medes were of the same race as the Persians, but their clothes were somewhat different, for whereas Persian garments were close-fitting and of comparatively thick materials, those of the Medes were more voluminous and made of thin stuffs. Persian women tended to adopt Median styles; formerly there had been little difference between their clothes and those of their husbands, except that the women's coats were wider and longer. The Median head-gear consisted of a hood covering the head, surrounding the face and concealing the chin. An alternative was a round cap with a flat crown and wider at the top than at the bottom.

8   Much of the unsettled land of the Middle East at this time was peopled by wild tribes

of Scythians, famous horsemen living a semi-nomadic existence which gave little opportunity for the development of luxury in dress. Their flocks and herds supplied them with wool and leather and by hunting they obtained furs, very necessary in the cold winters of the steppes over which they roamed. The cut of their clothes was both primitive and practical. The men wore trousers and a short coat open in front which was sometimes tucked into the trousers and sometimes left free. They had short top-coats and on their heads a piece of cloth kept in position with string, or a cap resembling the Phrygian cap already described. The women's dress was the same in essentials as that of the men, but the coats were longer and wider and decorated with embroidery.

The most formidable Scythian tribe was that of the Parthians, famous for their horsemanship and skill in archery. Their trousers were the same as those worn by all the Scythians, but their coats, no doubt owing to their closer contact with Persian civilization, were softer and more highly coloured with extremely long sleeves. Parthian women were sometimes very richly adorned, characteristic features being the bows of ribbon down the front of the dress, and the veil fastened to the head and falling down the back.

Other tribes, such as the Sarmatians, Dacians and Illyrians showed minor variations in costume. The Dacians, for example, were distinguished by their long cloaks, semicircular in form, and having curved edges adorned with fringes. Both Dacians and Illyrians wore a rather stiff felt cap of the shape which has come down to our time as the tarboosh, abolished in Turkey a generation ago, but still worn in Egypt and other Arab countries. It is an example of the extraordinary persistence of fashion in that part of the world.

9

10   **Spartan Costume,** *c.* 500 B.C. *From the statuette in the British Museum.*

CHAPTER TWO

The Greeks and Romans

Until comparatively recently the study of Greek costume was confined to so-called classical times beginning about the sixth century B.C. By the researches of Sir Arthur Evans and other archæologists in Crete and on the mainland, however, a much earlier civilization was revealed, dating back to the period 2000 to 1500 B.C. The interesting thing is that the clothes worn by the Cretans and Minoans were quite different from those familiar to classical scholars. They were extremely elaborate, brightly coloured and gaily patterned.

Both men and women were remarkable for the extreme slenderness of the waist, a slenderness which could only have been produced by some kind of girdle worn from earliest youth. The effect is of a tight corset, something which was not to be seen again in European fashion until the close of the Middle Ages.

The men wore a tight loin-cloth and over it a kind of kilt patterned with zigzag stripes. This was usually short but could be worn longer, especially by older men and in court dress. It was ornamented with a fringe. On the Greek mainland, where the climate could be severe in winter, a cloak was worn in addition. Sandals and high boots of soft white leather protected the feet. The hair was worn very long, sometimes twisted into knots on the top of the head. Hats were not usual but metal helmets, sometimes with crests, were worn in battle.

It is thought that the loin-cloth was worn by women as well as men, with a fantastic arrangement of skirts over it, constructed in tiers of flounces, with a rounded apron on top. The upper part of the body was clad in a little sleeved jacket cut so low as to expose the breasts. Except for the last characteristic, the whole outfit was more like a fashionable dress of the mid-nineteenth century than any intervening mode. Strangely enough, women's hair was cut much shorter than men's, but it was usually visible under the head-dress which might take the form of a high, conical cap, a horned hat or a kind of flat turban.

11

Sometimes a fillet of gold like a tiara was worn, and there was a considerable amount of jewellery in the form of necklaces of gold and lapis lazuli (azure stone). Gold hairpins have been found in both male and female Minoan tombs.

The highly-developed Minoan civilization was brought to an end about 1500 B.C. by the invading Dorians from the north, and, after a long period of confusion, a new civilization arose, the civilization we can recognize as Greek. Fortunately we know a great deal about it, owing to the wealth of statuary that has come down to us. Much evidence, especially from the earlier period, can also be obtained from vase paintings, and there are many references to costume in Homer.

It is generally agreed that what is called Hellenic costume (that is, the dress of the Greek classical period) differed from the pre-Hellenic costume we have been describing, in that it was entirely draped; that is, it consisted of pieces of material of simple form suspended from the body by means of pins or brooches. It is thought that the Trojan War was, actually, fought in pre-Hellenic costume; or it is possible that the Trojans represented the old civilization and wore clothes similar to those of the Cretans, and that the Greeks were the invaders from the north and wore costumes of the draped type. The Homeric poems contain many descriptions of the dress of both men and women but they were composed centuries after the events they describe. Homer, therefore, puts *all* his characters into Greek dress, which by this time had established itself, the very memory of the older civilization having faded away.

From the seventh to the first century B.C. the principal item of clothing worn by both men and women was the *chiton*. Men wore it knee-length and women ankle-length. It consisted of a rectangle of material hung on the shoulders by means of pins or brooches in such a way as to form a tunic which was usually confined at the waist with a cord. In its earliest form it consisted of two rectangular pieces of the same size, sewn together like a sack, but with openings for the head and arms. The later *chiton* of the fifth and fourth centuries could be made in two forms, narrow or wide, the latter giving a greater fullness of material and falling in more graceful folds. Sometimes two cords were fastened round the waist, giving the effect of a double girdle.

Over the *chiton* women wore the *peplos* which also consisted of a rectangle of material attached in a similar way. Instead of this, men—especially young men and horsemen—wore over the *chiton* a kind of cloak called a *chlamys*, fastened usually on one shoulder. Sometimes the *chlamys* was worn by itself, and as the Greeks had no horror of nudity or semi-nudity this mode was accepted. In cold weather a much larger cloak was worn by both sexes. This was known as the *himation*, and consisted of an oblong piece of material about seven or eight feet in length and as wide as the wearer's height. It could be worn in many ways: as a head covering, or a cloak, or draped over the shoulders like a shawl.

Out of all these simple garments an enormous variety of costumes could be contrived. The *peplos* could be closed at one side and given an over-fold falling to the waist. The girdle could be worn over this or underneath it; the long, open *chiton* could be sleeved or sleeveless; the over-fold could be long or short. Indeed the Greek woman could provide herself with a whole wardrobe of dresses all constructed from single rectangles of plain cloth. In the early days, however (sixth century B.C.), the materials were gaily patterned, as can

13

Athenian Male Costume, *c.* 480 B.C. *From a figured amphora in the British Museum.*

be seen from vase paintings of the period, and we can perhaps look upon this as a relic of Minoan influence which gradually faded away.

Scholars distinguish between two types of *chiton*, the Doric and the Ionic—the former being fastened by means of pins or brooches, the latter being sewn—but that this was not always so can be seen from many examples in sculpture and vase painting. The real distinction lay in the sleeves, the Doric *chiton* being sleeveless. The Doric *chiton* was made of wool, the Ionic usually of linen, allowing for more numerous and more delicate folds. The latter was longer than the height of the wearer, the superfluous material being pulled up through the girdle to give a blouse effect. The simplest form of the Ionic *chiton* is plainly shown in the famous statue known as the Charioteer of Delphi, now in the Delphi Museum, but this long type, although worn by men, was more typical of female dress. The sleeves could be pinned or sewn. Sometimes *chitons* are found on vase paintings with full sleeves to the elbow, and these were presumably formed in the modern manner by sewing the sleeves on separately. They could originally have been in one piece with the dress, but this would have required the material to be cut in the form of a cross, with consequent waste. We can thus see the beginning of tailoring or dressmaking, in a costume which was essentially draped.

The upper part of the Ionic *chiton* was loose and was often kept in place by means of cross-bands and shoulder-cords, usually attached to the girdle. Sometimes a second, rather high girdle was worn or, alternatively, a broad band under the breasts, serving the purpose of a modern corset. The *himation* when worn by women over the *chiton* could be of very fine material and an article of luxury. Indeed, luxury gradually crept in, even to the wearing of materials so fine as to be almost transparent, in spite of the efforts of rulers like Solon to control women's dress by law. Silk was increasingly used by fashionable women.

It was at one time supposed that since nearly all the Greek statues that have survived are unpainted, they must have been so in their original condition. Further discoveries, especially of earlier examples, have negatived this idea, and helped to dispose of the notion that actual Greek clothes were invariably white or of the natural colour of wool or flax. It is probable that only slaves and the lowest classes of artisans wore clothes of plain materials, and even these were sometimes embellished with a border. The clothes of the upper classes showed considerable colour and patterning. The favourite colours were purple, red and yellow. Green and grey are also mentioned by ancient writers, but, strangely enough, no blue.

Sometimes the ornamentation consisted of a simple border; sometimes the whole dress was patterned. Examples of patterned Greek materials which have been found in tombs show that designs were often geometric or floral, though animals and human figures are also found. Usually figures and patterns were embroidered on to rather than woven into the cloth; in a few cases they appear to have been painted on.

Hairdressing shows considerable variation in the course of Greek history. In pre-Hellenic times, and even up to the time of the Persian wars, both men and women wore their hair long. From about the middle of the fifth century B.C. most men cut their hair short and women bound it up. It became customary for youths to cut off their hair on attaining manhood and dedicate it to the gods, and long hair in men was considered a sign of effeminacy or foppishness. Beards were usual up to the fifth century B.C. but after this were only worn by old men and by those philosophers who prided themselves on living the simple life. Hats, which were broad-brimmed felts, were hardly ever worn except for travelling and even then, except in very wet or very hot weather, they were often carried on the shoulder rather than worn on the head, being regarded more as umbrellas or parasols than hats. Sailors are sometimes depicted with felt caps of conical shape without brims, rather like the tarboosh or fez.

Even before the Persian wars women sometimes held their hair in place with a ribbon or even a metal band. When it was 'done-up' the back hair was frequently enclosed in a kind of bag like a chignon worn low on the nape of the neck. Sometimes the hair was enclosed in a kerchief either entirely concealing it or allowing a few curls to escape. In the fourth century B.C. the chignon was worn higher up the head, and sometimes projected backward to a point. By the time of Alexander the Great, and especially after the Roman conquest, hairdressing styles became very numerous—curled, frizzed and artificial hair being frequently worn. Statues of goddesses often show a diadem or tiara of precious metal set with jewels, and we may assume that such ornaments were worn by the wealthy. Out of doors some women (as can be seen in the statuettes in the British Museum) drew veils over their heads and wore on top straw hats of peculiar form, something like small umbrellas.

It is thought that nearly all the Greeks went barefoot indoors, but in the street the upper classes wore various kinds of footgear. The simplest form was the sandal consisting of a leather sole fastened on by means of thongs. Sometimes the sandal had a back and sides of leather leaving only the toes exposed. From this developed the slipper which covered the foot completely. There was also a high boot probably of Asiatic origin used on journeys and by soldiers. These sometimes had nails on the soles, and it is surprising to learn from the playwright Aristophanes that blacking was in use. It was made of pitch and applied with a sponge.

The Etruscans, whose civilization in Italy preceded that of Rome, were for long a mysterious people, but archæologists have now discovered enough about them to show that their earliest costume somewhat resembled that of pre-Hellenic Crete. The basic article of dress was a shirt-like garment similar to the Greek *chiton*, and, over it, they wore a kind of cloak, called a *tebenna*, sometimes rectangular and sometimes semicircular. The women's dress was more Oriental consisting of a long robe tight-fitting over the shoulders and growing gradually wider, worn without a girdle. It had half-length sleeves. A slit at the back, sometimes fastened with ribbons, enabled the garment to be put on over the head. It was thus quite different in structure from contemporary Greek dress. Over the robe Etruscan women wore a long, rectangular cloak sometimes arranged as a shawl over the shoulders and sometimes drawn over the head.

Much more is known of Roman costume. In its earliest form male dress consisted of a kind of shirt known as a *tunica* and a cloak worn over it. This was the *toga*, the most characteristic Roman garment. In its simplest state it was a fairly small square of cloth but it could assume enormous proportions, and in its typical form consisted of two segments of

16   **Greek Female Costume, fourth century** B.C.

a circle joined along the straight edges; or it could be made of a single piece of material of the same shape. It was put on by folding the material about the middle, then gathering the ends and throwing them over the left shoulder so that they hung in thick folds down the back. In mourning and for certain religious ceremonies the *toga* could be draped over the head. Since it was usually immensely voluminous and made any active pursuit impossible, it was a typical garment of the upper classes. When worn by senators it was always white, its whiteness being sometimes accentuated by the application of chalk. Certain officials wore it with a purple border, as did also freeborn boys until they attained to manhood. The *toga prætexta*, as it was called, was then put off at a ceremony attended by the family and friends of the youth, and the plain *toga virilis* (or manly *toga*) assumed. In mourning a dark-coloured *toga* was worn, while the one worn by those who had been accorded a Triumph for their services to the state was decorated with coloured patterns. The Emperor Augustus made this patterned *toga* the official costume of his court.

The *tunica* worn under the *toga*, or by itself, was a kind of shirt usually reaching to below the knee. Soldiers, however, wore it above the knee and bridegrooms down to the ground. It sometimes had elbow-length sleeves. The hardy Romans of the Republic wore only one *tunica* but, later, two were worn, and long-sleeved tunics which had formerly only been worn by foreign priests and actors were gradually adopted. The Romans did not wear breeches or trews and were actually long forbidden to do so. Trousers were the typical garments of the northern tribes against whom the Romans were defending their frontier, and were therefore despised as barbaric. Nevertheless they gradually made their way, being adopted by the legionaries who had to fight in comparatively cold climates. At first the Roman breeches were short and tight, but in the later Empire they became wider and sometimes reached to the ankles—trousers, in fact—but these were never fashionable. In bad weather the Romans wore a kind of bell-shaped cloak called a *pænula* which was usually provided with a hood. Hats were not worn by civilians although, of course, helmets were provided for soldiers.

In the early, austere days female dress was hardly distinguishable from that worn by men. Sometimes only one *tunica* was worn, closed all round except for the armholes. It had short sleeves, and was made first of wool, then of linen, and then, with the growth of luxury, of silk. Over the tunic the Roman lady wore a similar garment usually with sleeves, known as a *stola*, and over this, when she went out, she put on a *pella*, a voluminous cloak rather like a *toga* but square or oblong in shape. A veil was usually worn in public, attached to the back of the head and hanging down the back.

Men wore their hair short and were clean-shaven until the time of the Emperor Hadrian who was bearded and set a new fashion. Women's hair was at first very simply dressed and covered with a veil, but once the power of Rome was established and the tribute of sub-jugated peoples began to flow in, luxury of all kinds became commonplace. Head-gear in particular grew increasingly elaborate, and for the simple bandeaux borrowed from the Greeks, the Roman ladies substituted broad bands of stuff embroidered in gold and adorned with pearls and cameos. The hair itself was elaborately twisted and curled, and many of the head-dresses could only have been obtained by considerable skill with the curling iron.

There is a wealth of evidence in Roman portrait busts of the quick changes of hair-

17

Roman Civil Costume, first century B.C.

dressing styles, and it is recorded that some Roman ladies were so determined that even their portraits should continue to be in the fashion that the sculptured hair was made separately from the rest of the bust and could be changed when desired. Hairpins and combs made their appearance, some of them of gold or ivory, and much false hair was obtained from the Gaulish and Germanic tribes. This often had the advantage of being

18

naturally light in colour, blond hair being admired by the Romans. The natural hair was frequently bleached and Ovid, in one of his poems, warns a girl of his acquaintance that the excessive use of bleaches might result in baldness.

As Christianity made its way in the Roman world such vanities were increasingly frowned upon. Even the plaiting of hair was denounced. Christian women accordingly wore veils almost entirely concealing the hair, but as most of them belonged at first to the humbler classes, this did not have much immediate influence on fashion.

Constantine, the first Christian Emperor, moved the capital from Rome to Byzantium, or Constantinople, where Europe and Asia met. It was therefore to be expected that the clothes of both men and women would show increasing signs of Oriental influence, and that the last traces of the old Roman simplicity would disappear. Byzantine clothes, with their damask patterns woven in silk and gold thread, had a stiff magnificence which was something new in the history of fashion. The Emperor Theodosius (A.D. 379 to A.D. 395) introduced a degree of magnificence which was continued by all the Eastern rulers after him. Silk was much used. Formerly it had had to be imported from China, but in the time of the Emperor Justinian (A.D. 527 to A.D. 565) it was found possible to rear silkworms in Europe, and although silk remained an article of luxury it was increasingly employed by wealthy people.

It is curious that from the time of the establishment of the Roman Eastern Empire it is almost impossible to distinguish between male and female costume. The grandest clothes were, of course, reserved for the Imperial pair. Over the tunic, which now had narrow sleeves to the wrist and was itself of rich material, was worn the mantle, embroidered in gold and sometimes sewn all over with pearls or other jewels. At the front, waist-high, was an oblong band known as a *tablion*, even more elaborately embroidered. The Empress wore this also, from the sixth century onwards. The colour of the Imperial mantle was always purple. It was suspended from the right shoulder by means of a jewelled ornament. The similar mantle was worn by women. Sometimes the *tunica* was replaced by the *dalmatica*, the distinctive feature of which was its wide sleeves. It was originally unbelted but was later worn with a belt low over the hips.

The Greeks and Romans

We can gain considerable information concerning the Imperial costume in the sixth century from the splendid mosaics in the churches at Ravenna. In San Vitale both the Emperor Justinian and the Empress Theodora are shown, and their costumes blaze with gold embroidery and jewels. The Emperor, it is interesting to note, is wearing hose, presumably of silk, and closed shoes instead of sandals. The nobles attendant on the Imperial pair are only slightly less richly clad. It goes without saying that, outside court circles, plainer garments were worn but they were of the same general form.

Women's head-dresses from the beginning of the fifth century show marked Oriental influences. The hair was dressed in a circular roll or pad with a close-fitting cap inside it. Above the roll and hiding the cap was a jewelled coronet, or, in the case of the Empress, a crown. The same form of head-dress, without the jewels, was gradually adopted by women of the middle classes and lasted for several centuries. Byzantine court costume is important because of its influence on the dress of royalty all over Europe and also on the development of ecclesiastical vestments. The clergy of the Orthodox Church wear the trappings of Byzantium to this day.

19

Galla Placidia, Regent of the
West, A.D. 430.

20

CHAPTER THREE

The Dark Ages

When the power of Rome began to decline, the barbarian peoples who lived around its borders began to make inroads into the imperial territory. They had attempted to do so for many centuries, and had defeated a Roman army as early as 113 B.C. This is the first we hear of the Teutoni or Teutons. They inhabited the region of the lower Elbe and in the first century A.D. the Roman centurion Tacitus refers to their country as Germania.

In their early days the Teutons were naked savages but later adopted a kind of short tunic made of two pieces of skin sewn together at the shoulders and down the sides. Later these garments were made of wool or linen. It was not until the second century A.D. that they began to bind pieces of skin on their feet as primitive shoes. They seem to have worn some kind of hose or breeches as far back as the Bronze Age. These sometimes reached to the ankles but specimens have been found, preserved in peat in various parts of Germany, resembling our modern shorts.

The women, clad in skins, like the men, gradually became more civilized and by the beginning of the Christian era were wearing an approximation to Roman dress except that the cloth was of hemp instead of wool. They wore the long Roman tunic and the semi-circular cloak and were fond of decorating both with stripes, spots and even animals and birds. They had fair hair, usually worn loose about the shoulders. The men too paid great attention to their hair, sometimes dyeing it red. Elaborate combs and pins have been found in Teutonic tombs.

The Goths came originally from Gothland, that is, Scandinavia, but by the end of the first century A.D. they were settled (if such a word can be applied to them) round the mouth of the Vistula in the region later to be known as East Prussia. In the third century A.D. they pushed southwards, crossed the Danube and raided the Balkans. There were several tribes of Goths, the most famous being the Ostrogoths who went eastward to

21

what is now Russia, the Langobards (or Longbeards) who, starting from the region of Hanover, finally settled in the north of Italy, giving their name to Lombardy, and the Visigoths who pushed west to Spain. The most famous leader of the Visigoths was Alaric who sacked Rome three times at the beginning of the fifth century.

Roman historians have left descriptions of the costume of the Goths. According to Sidonius Apollinaris their principal garment was a linen tunic with sleeves, sometimes edged with fur. On their head was a hood rather like the Phrygian cap already mentioned. At first their legs were bare but they later adopted long trousers, sometimes cross-gartered. Their contacts with Rome led them gradually to adopt Roman fashions and, after the fifth century, they were much impressed by the gorgeous modes of the Eastern Empire. They wore beards and curled their long hair.

These Teutonic tribes had themselves to face the peril of invasion from the East, especially by the Huns. The original home of the Huns was in Mongolia, but they were a nomadic people and, after threatening the Chinese Empire during the third century B.C., turned westward, and by the middle of the first century A.D. were settled in Europe round the Caspian Sea. In the fourth century they broke into the Balkans, and under Attila threatened Rome itself. Their clothing was primitive, consisting of a single tunic, made, for the more prosperous, of cloth woven from the hair of the camel or the yak. The poorer Huns and slaves had tunics of coarse hemp made from fibrous bark. Fur was much used, a simple pelt being flung over the shoulders as a cloak. Caps were bright in colour and edged with fur. The legs and arms were bare and the primitive shoes were of the moccasin type.

The Romans finally departed from Britain about 450 A.D. and the country soon became the prey of the invading Angles, Jutes and Saxons. The romanized Britons were wearing a provincial version of Roman costume, but the newcomers were more barbarously clad, and for long retained the styles of the lands from which they had come. This is shown quite clearly by excavations. Graves in the south of England contained relics identical with those found in the ancient graves of Saxony; the graves of the Angles and Jutes contained objects very similar to those found in Denmark. Much of what has been preserved is in the form of jewellery, notably the large *fibulæ* or clasps used for fastening the materials of the dress, but we can gain some idea of the invaders' costume from contemporary chronicles. The Angles and Saxons under Hengist and Horsa wore tunics of leather and 'four-cornered' (a puzzling phrase) helmets. Hengist himself had little scales of metal attached to his tunic to serve the purpose of armour and his cloak was the skin of a wild beast. He had primitive leather shoes like moccasins and his legs were bound round with leather straps. Some of the invaders wore the characteristic Teuton trousers, cross-gartered to the knees. Hair and beards were long.

Women wore a straight dress reaching to the ankles with short sleeves, and over this a kind of tunic, sometimes slit at the sides and belted at the waist. A second belt hung round the hips, richly decorated, with various objects suspended from it by chains. The hair was worn loose on the shoulders. Poorer women seem to have been content with a cloth skirt and a short jacket.

By the year A.D. 700 the country had begun to settle down again after centuries of tumult. It was now divided into the three kingdoms of Northumbria, Mercia and Wessex, and Offa

Charles the Bald, Emperor of the West, and the Emperor Lothair. *From a Bible in the Louvre. (After Jaquemin.)*

Norman Costume. *From the Bayeux Tapestry.*

made Mercia the most important and powerful of these. He maintained close relations with the Continent and sent English scholars including the famous Alcuin to the court of Charlemagne. Charlemagne was at this period the most important man in Europe. He became sole ruler of the Franks (that is, over the inhabitants of what is now, roughly, France and Germany) in A.D. 771 and in A.D. 800 he was crowned in St. Peter's, Rome, as Roman Emperor. So influential a man was widely acclaimed and copied throughout Europe and it is fortunate that we have a surprisingly detailed description of his costume from the hand of his secretary Eginhard. He says that Charlemagne usually dressed very simply. He wore an under-tunic of linen and braies or breeches cross-gartered to below the knee. Over these he wore an over-tunic of linen or woollen material sometimes edged with a border of coloured silk. Attached to the left shoulder by means of a brooch he wore a short semicircular cloak bordered and lined with silk in summer and with fur in winter. On his head he wore a round cloth cap with an embroidered headband.

Very different was his appearance as Emperor. His costume had nothing of the Ancient Roman about it; it was plainly modelled on the Byzantine style and consisted of a tunic with narrow sleeves edged with gold, and over this a wide sleeved *dalmatica* (which had now become an almost entirely ecclesiastical garment and here symbolized the Emperor's protection of the Church). Over this was a variety of elaborate garments, heavily embroidered in gold and one of them made of brocade manufactured in Constantinople and patterned with large floriated circles of green, blue and gold, enclosing figures of elephants. Another garment was of cloth of gold, brocaded in squares with a ruby or an emerald set in the centre of each. He wore shoes of scarlet leather embroidered with gold and set with emeralds; and on his head was a splendid gold crown adorned with enamelled plaques and jewels. When his tomb at Aachen was opened in the twelfth century he was found seated on an ivory throne and clad in these Imperial robes, small fragments of which have been preserved until this day.

The Dark Ages

Charlemagne himself did not care for luxury and issued several edicts against extravagance in dress, but his successors, both kings of France and emperors of Germany (for the union of the two countries did not long survive his death) dressed as richly as possible, drawing much of the material for their costumes from the factories of the Eastern Empire. In contrast the English kings were comparatively simply clad. We know, for example, from an illuminated manuscript now in the library of Corpus Christi College, Cambridge, that King Athelstan wore a plain, short yellow tunic with a narrow gold border, a blue cloak and red hose. King Edgar wore a similar costume, though it was shorter, revealing his knees, his legs being enclosed in narrow bands rather like puttees. This information is obtained from a document concerning the grant in A.D. 966 of lands and privileges to the Abbey of Winchester (now in the British Museum), written in letters of gold and illustrated with drawings of Edgar in the costume described.

The costume of Anglo-Saxon nobles was not very different except for the absence of the crown. Instead a kind of Phrygian cap was sometimes worn, but most men went about bare-headed. An ealdorman—literally, an older man—a member of the King's council or witenagemot, wore a conical cap as a mark of his office and a long tunic reaching to the ankles. The hair of men of all ages was worn fairly long, with a centre parting and tucked

25

behind the ears. The beard was rather like the naval type of beard of recent times but was sometimes longer and forked. The dress of the humbler classes was essentially the same as that of the nobles but made of coarser materials and without embroidered borders.

Fortunately, from illuminated manuscripts that have come down to us, we know a considerable amount about the dress of Anglo-Saxon women. The principal garment was the *gunna* or gown which reached, unbelted, from neck to ankles. It had fairly wide elbow-length sleeves and was often ornamented with a band of embroidery round the neck, round the sleeves and vertically down the front. The Anglo-Saxons were famous for their embroidery, worked in gold, silver and coloured silk threads. It was indeed the principal occupation of ladies of the upper classes. The patterns were Byzantine in origin. Under the gown another was worn of about the same shape but with tight-fitting sleeves to the wrist, and under this again a long linen garment called a *camise* (that is, a chemise). The head was covered by a square veil of semi-transparent material and a semicircular cloak hung from the shoulders. In the ninth century a new kind of veil was introduced. It consisted of a circle of material with a circular hole cut, not in the centre but about a third of the way across. The veil was draped over the head in such a way that the face and throat appeared through the hole.

As women of this period are nearly always shown with veils on their heads it is difficult to know how the hair was dressed. Ornamental hairpins have been found, however, in considerable numbers, so that the hair was presumably pinned up round the head in some simple way. Young girls wore it long and loose over their shoulders, with a band to keep it from being too unruly. In the privacy of their homes women of all classes wore their

hair in the same way.

When the Danes invaded the country and finally succeeded in establishing themselves as its rulers, what chiefly distinguished them from the Anglo-Saxons was the length of their hair. The hair of King Canute is described as hanging thick over his shoulders, and some of his courtiers had hair descending to their waists. They bestowed much attention on it, combing it once a day. Otherwise they differed little in appearance from the Anglo-Saxons except that their garments were traditionally black. The invading forces were known as the 'Black Army' and the raven was their chosen emblem. Later they abandoned this peculiarity and adopted the English range of colours: greys, dark greens and browns. As the dyers depended on vegetable dyes and earth colours, garments, except for embroidered ones, were rather sombre.

Another Danish peculiarity was the wearing of bracelets by men. They were made of gold or bronze and were bestowed for bravery in battle, as a kind of equivalent to the medals of later days. One of the Kings is described as 'Lord of Earls, bracelet-giver to heroes', so that the custom was universally recognized. Jewellery was not much worn, although King Alfred had encouraged foreign goldsmiths to settle in England, and some of the work produced by native craftsmen was very fine. King Alfred's Jewel, now in the British Museum, is a skilful blend of gold and enamel. Necklaces of gold chains and twisted wire-work set with precious stones have come down to us but it is unlikely that they were much worn by Anglo-Saxon women as the veil would have obscured them from view.

Ear-rings were very small and usually plain, but some of the finger-rings of twisted wire

William Rufus. *From a miniature in the Bibliothèque St. Geneviève. (After Jacquemin.)*

3

27

were quite elaborate in form and were probably derived from Byzantine models. The most spectacular pieces of jewellery were the buckles and ornamental pins used for attaching the cloak.

And now another influence began to make itself felt. On the other side of the Channel the Northmen who had established themselves in what had now become the Dukedom of Normandy had adopted French manners as well as the French language. When the Danish dynasty came to an end in England in A.D. 1042, Edward (known for his piety as the Confessor) was called to the throne. He was the son of Aethelred the Unready and Emma, daughter of the Duke of Normandy. He was therefore half Norman by descent; and, in addition, he had spent the greater part of his life, from the age of thirteen to the age of forty, in Normandy. F. W. Fairholt in his pioneer book *Costume in England* sums up the situation in words that could hardly be bettered:

His Norman predilections were visible in all he did; he spoke in their language, and introduced their customs into his palace, which was pretty nearly populated by Norman adventurers, whose company the King, from long habit, generally preferred. The Saxons, who desired to be well with their monarch, learned to speak French . . . and the dress, fashions and manners of the Normans were as faithfully imitated, much to the disgust of the genuine Saxon lords.

The accession of Harold made very little difference, for he himself had resided in Normandy and the monkish chroniclers of the time were loud in their complaints of the imitation of Norman modes. The English, they declared, 'had transformed themselves in speech and garb and adopted all that was ridiculous in the manner of that people. They shortened their tunics, they trimmed their hair, they loaded their arms with golden bracelets and entirely forgot their usual simplicity.' In spite of these accusations we can be pretty sure that Norman influences as yet extended little further than the court, but after the Norman Conquest, they naturally increased.

One of the most striking differences between Saxons and Normans was the habit the latter had of shaving not only the face but the back of the head. So startling was this novelty that the spies sent out by Harold before the Battle of Hastings reported that they had seen no soldiers but only priests. Unfortunately the 'priests' were more than a match for the Anglo-Saxon warriors.

We know a good deal about the costume of this period from what is known as the Bayeux Tapestry—which is really a piece of embroidery rather than a tapestry. It is perhaps most valuable for its representation of Norman armour which is outside the scope of the present work. It is plain that there were no striking differences between Norman and Saxon civilian costume. The Norman tunic was more close-fitting, and could be plain with a decorated border (this was more usual) or patterned all over. It was knee-length except for ceremonial occasions when it reached to the ankles and had a low round neck or a slit in front to enable it to be put on over the head. The sleeves were long, fairly wide at the shoulder but narrow at the wrists.

Over the tunic the super-tunic was worn, a garment of circular form with loose sleeves. It was usual to hitch up both garments with a girdle. The cloak consisted of a rectangular or semicircular piece of material fastened by a brooch on the shoulder. The cloaks of the nobility were often lined with fur. Breeches or braies were universally worn, usually

COSTUME

28

long, to the ankles. The upper classes wore them tight-fitting, the lower classes loose. Leg bandages of linen or wool, sometimes wound spirally like puttees and sometimes criss-crossed, were usual until the end of the eleventh century. Shoes were pointed and shaped to the foot, but without a heel. It was unusual to wear a hat, but a hood was sometimes attached to the cloak and could be pulled over the head in bad weather.

Over a chemise, women wore a gown, or kirtle, similar in form to the male tunic but always long, reaching to the ankles. Over this was the *roc*, similar to the super-tunic of the men. The cloak or mantle reached to the ground and was sometimes worn double. Women wore stockings or hose but nothing corresponding to the masculine braies. The head was covered by a kerchief entirely concealing the hair except in the case of young girls who wore their hair loose about the shoulders. Soon after the Conquest we begin to find denunciations of luxury, especially at the court of William Rufus, but by comparison with the costume of the Middle Ages, the clothes of the eleventh century seem simple indeed.

30

Female Costume, 1380. *From the brass in Cobham Church, Kent.*

CHAPTER FOUR

The Middle Ages

Between the Norman Conquest and the middle of the twelfth century there was little change in the costume of either men or women. Men continued to wear the tunic, the super-tunic and the cloak or mantle as their principal garments, and women the kirtle or gown. But the tunic of the nobility, from about 1130 onwards, began to be made with a tight-fitting body and the long skirt to be slit up the front to thigh-level and kept in place by a sword-belt. The cloak was sometimes small and lined with fur. About the middle of the century breeches were shortened to the knee, and soon became undergarments. Hose, which could be either short, ending below the knee, or long, reaching to mid-thigh, were often fitted with a thin leather sole, which made it unnecessary to wear shoes. Sometimes the hose themselves were made of leather, King John having a pair of cowhide.

The characteristic head-gear, lasting for three centuries, was the hood. It was usually in the form of a pointed cowl attached to a cape over the shoulders. Hats also were worn for travelling and had wide brims and low crowns. The hood, however, was frequently worn underneath. Under this again, from the end of the twelfth century to the middle of the fourteenth, was worn the coif, a close-fitting bonnet of linen which covered the ears and was tied under the chin. It resembled a baby's bonnet. Usually men's hair was long and beards and moustaches were quite common, although young men tended to be clean-shaven and have short hair.

Women's hair was entirely covered either by the veil or the wimple, which concealed everything but the face. Sometimes the face itself was partially hidden, by the *barbette*, a linen band passing over the chin. Royal ladies and others of high rank, from about A.D. 1120, sometimes had two long plaits of hair descending in front of the shoulders to the knees. False hair was used by those whose natural hair was not long enough.

We know a good deal about royal costume at the end of the twelfth century from the effigies of English kings and queens. Those of Henry II and Eleanor of Guienne, and that of Richard I are still to be seen at the Abbey of Fontevraud in France, and that of King John in Worcester Cathedral. Henry II wears a mantle of a deep reddish-brown colour and under it a dalmatic, or super-tunic, of crimson patterned with gold stars or flowers. The boots are green with gold edging and the gloves have large jewels fastened upon the backs. His queen, Eleanor of Guienne, wears a long gown with a close collar, fastened round the waist with a jewelled girdle. It is patterned with golden crescents. The under-tunic is visible at the neck where it is fastened with a circular brooch. Richard I has a blue mantle edged with gold, a red dalmatic and a white tunic, and below this a white shirt. King John wears a similar costume but the garments are shorter.

The effigy of King Henry III is in Westminster Abbey and is remarkable for the comparative simplicity of the costume. The boots are scarlet and patterned with gold squares each containing the figure of a lion, but no ornament is to be seen on either the cloak or the dalmatic. This plainness probably represented Henry III's personal taste, for many rich stuffs were beginning to be imported at this time, even from as far away as Damascus (from which we get the word damask) and Babylon. The Crusades had made the West familiar with such Oriental luxuries.

Edward I is reported to have dressed always in an unostentatious manner. No monumental effigy of him exists, but he was buried in Westminster Abbey and when his tomb was opened in 1774 the body was found clothed in a dalmatic of red silk damask, with a crimson mantle, and a stole of white tissue ornamented with gold and knots of pearls. The lower part of the body was swathed in cloth of gold.

In spite of his personal tastes Edward I had done much to introduce luxurious styles to England. In 1298 he married the sister of Philip IV of France, nicknamed *le Bel* (or, as we would say, the Beau), and his son married the daughter of the same monarch. All this made for the introduction of French modes, and when the son succeeded to the throne as Edward II he encouraged a degree of luxury which disgusted the English nobles and was partly the cause of his dethronement and death.

The shape of garments, however continued unaltered until about the year 1340, in the middle of the reign of Philip of Valois in France, when there was a striking change. The long tunics and super-tunics were given up in favour of shorter garments moulded to the figure, the long, tight hose being now visible. It is thought by some that the new fashion came from Spain, but it seems to have been adopted almost simultaneously in France, Italy and England.

The new male costume consisted mainly of a *gipon*, later called a doublet (a kind of short tunic, tight-fitting and buttoned down the front) and a *cote-hardie* which replaced the super-tunic and was worn over the *gipon*. It too was close-fitting and reached to the knees. The girdle was worn below waist-level, round the hips. Above the *cote-hardie* could be worn the *garnache*, a garment resembling a tabard (as still worn by heralds at a modern Coronation) but with shoulder-line wide enough to fall down to the elbows, producing the effect of wide, short sleeves.

In the last quarter of the fourteenth century a new garment came into use. It was known as the *houppelande* until about 1450, after which it was called a gown. In its

33

Male Costume, *c.* **1405.** *From the brass in Holme-by-the-Sea Church, Norfolk.*

34

Female Costume, 1419. *From the brass in Hever Church, Kent.*

ceremonial form (as seen, for example, in royal effigies) it reached to the ankles, but it was often worn knee-length. It fitted over the shoulders and fell below the waist in voluminous pleats. In its original form it was put on over the head, but from about 1400 it was sometimes buttoned down the front. The curious thing about it was its high collar reaching to the ears and standing up at the back. This was generally dagged, and dagging is so usual a feature of clothes at this period that it must be described in some detail. It appears about 1350 and lasts until the end of the fifteenth century. It consisted in cutting the border of a garment in the shape of leaves or tongues. The parson, in Chaucer's *Canterbury Tales* denounces it as sinful extravagance, but as all new fashions have been similarly denounced by moralists, this need not surprise us. The sleeves of the gown were enormously wide at the wrists and edges frequently dagged.

The upper classes were now wearing tight-fitting hose made of stretchable material, cut on the cross, with a seam down the back: knitted hose did not come into use until the second half of the sixteenth century. The legs could be of different colours, as could the different sides of the *gipon* or other garment. In a contemporary illuminated manuscript, John of Gaunt is shown in a gown, blue on one side and white on the other, these being the colours of the House of Lancaster. Sometimes not only symbolic colours were used but also heraldic emblems of all kinds, so that a fine lady and gentleman and their retainers frequently carried, so to speak, their coat of arms on their own persons.

Perhaps the most striking element in costume around the year 1400 is the footwear. Shoes had begun to be pointed as early as 1360, and a law was enacted by Edward III to help restrain them from becoming more so. This laid down that 'no Knight under the estate of a lord, esquire or gentleman, nor any other person, shall wear any shoes or boots having spikes or points exceeding the length of two inches, under the forfeiture of forty pence' (a considerable sum in those days). The statutory two inches was soon exceeded in the following reign. Richard II married Anne of Bohemia and the gentlemen of her suite wore extremely pointed shoes. These were called *crackowes*, from the city of Cracow, or *poulains*, a corruption of Poland, Poland being at that time part of the dominions of the Bohemian crown. The clergy denounced these too as 'devil's claws', and although we may reject this sinister suggestion, we must admit that the fashion must have been an extremely inconvenient one. The odd thing is that it was copied in armour, and this must have made it very difficult for an unmounted knight to walk.

Another curious feature of male costume at this period was the way in which the hood began to be worn. The opening, instead of framing the face, was fitted on to the head, the folds of what had been the cape being kept in place by winding round them the *liripipe*, which was the long point at the back of the hood. The dagged edges gave the appearance of a cockscomb, not erect on the head but hanging down on one side. Later, this arrangement was made permanent by stitching so that the whole contraption could be put on like a hat. Another form of head-gear was the turban, consisting of a length of cloth wound round the head.

There is a particular interest in women's clothes at this period for, from about 1360 onwards, we can see the beginnings of something we can recognize as fashion: a succession of rapidly changing modes. We can follow these changes not only from illuminated manuscripts (comparatively few of which have come down to us) but from the memorial brasses in churches which, in spite of the destruction wrought by later ages, can still be frequently seen. A brass is an incised design in a flat sheet of brass sunk into the surface of a stone slab. A rubbing can be taken of this and the result is a kind of primitive fashion-plate. There are large collections of such rubbings in museums, particularly in the Victoria and Albert Museum in London, and they form an invaluable record, especially as nearly all memorial brasses are dated.

It is not always realized that fashion, in the modern sense, is a comparatively recent idea. In the luxurious courts of France and Burgundy, in the middle of the fourteenth century, there was a sudden fresh realization that women's clothes, instead of being mere wrappings, could be potent weapons to attract and influence the other sex, and in little more than a decade the three devices upon which fashion has played infinite variations ever since were evolved. These three devices were *décolletage*, tight-lacing and striking head-dresses. Instead of the main garment being loose and enveloping, it was cut to reveal the shape of the figure and, in particular, to emphasize the smallness of the waist. Corsets had not yet been invented but the dress was stiffened with buckram to give very much the same effect. Instead of the top of the dress concealing the throat, it was cut away to reveal much of the bosom, and instead of the veil being used to cover the hair and a considerable portion of the face, it was drawn away from the countenance with pins and wires and even built up in a towering construction shaped like a church steeple or the devil's horns.

Of course, fashion started in courtly circles and had, for a long time, little effect on the dress of ordinary people, but the wives of prosperous citizens began, in spite of sumptuary laws, to copy the court ladies, and by the beginning of the fifteenth century we can say that every 'lady' knew what fashion was and followed it as best she could. Such an acceptance of change is the beginning of modernity. It is the emergence of the mobile modern world from the static world of the early Middle Ages.

Women continued, in the second half of the fourteenth century, to wear the kirtle or gown. It had a close-fitting bodice and full skirt and the girdle, like that worn by men, was round the hips. Sleeves were fitted closely and buttoned from the elbow to the hand. Sometimes they were continued beyond the wrists, giving the impression of mittens. The *cote-hardie* was still worn but the short flaps of the sleeves were lengthened to become streamers or tippets, sometimes trailing on the ground. A garment of increasing importance was the sideless surcoat, with large side-openings from shoulders to hips. It was often edged with fur. The front of the garment was known as a plackard. Women's shoes were never as long and pointed as those worn by men.

Fashion changes are most easily seen in the varying styles of head-dress. Older women continued to wear veils and wimples, but the more fashionable adopted various modes. Between 1350 and 1420 they wore what is called a goffered (or crinkled) veil or nebula head-dress. This consisted of a semicircle of linen with a broad goffered frill like a ruff, forming an arch round the face. This style has survived until today in the head-dresses worn by certain orders of nuns. Another variety was formed by two side-pieces covered with lattice-work, attached to a fillet worn on top of the head. Sometimes a padded roll

Male and Female Costume, late fourteenth century. *From* Roman de la Rose,
British Museum.

Portrait of a Young Lady, 1569. *From the painting in the Tate Gallery.*

was worn over a hair-net, and hair-nets or crespines in various shapes formed part of most head-dresses.

In the fifteenth century many elaborate forms of head-gear were developed, the effect being usually one of width until about 1450 and of height from that date until 1485. *Templers* were little latticed pads containing the hair worn at the temples with a veil descending from them to reach the shoulders. Sometimes the *templers* were twice as wide (measured together) as the width of the face. There were horned head-dresses and heart-shaped head-dresses. The hair was entirely concealed except by queens at their coronations, brides at their weddings and young girls generally. Sometimes the veils were wired to stand out from the head, the hair being enclosed in a net and forming bosses above the ears. There was a curious fashion of shaving off the eyebrows and the hair on the forehead.

In the second half of the fifteenth century, up to 1485, the most usual form was the butterfly head-dress which consisted of a veil of diaphanous material supported on a wire frame and often reaching enormous proportions. Other varieties were the turban head-dress, the cap in the shape of an inverted flowerpot and (in France, but not in England) the *hennin* or steeple head-dress.

The most striking change in men's appearance in the early years of the fifteenth century was due to the development of defensive armour. The helmet was now made with a chin-piece instead of the chain-mail cowl attached to the helmet. It therefore became necessary to shave off the beard which would have fitted very uncomfortably into the new style of helmet. Men also cut their hair short, and after 1410 they shaved it in a sharp line about the top of the ears in a 'bowl-crop'. This can be seen quite plainly in contemporary portraits of Henry V.

Men still wore the *gipon*, now increasingly known as a doublet, but from about 1420 it began to develop a collar. The characteristic garment of this period, however, was the *houppelande* or gown which now began to exhibit some important variations. It could be either long or short, sometimes so short that it barely covered the thighs. It was arranged in rigid folds rather like organ pipes, and was sometimes quilted. It could have a very tall 'bottle-neck' collar usually dagged, giving the appearance of a ruff. The sleeves were of several types nearly all of great size: funnel shaped, or shaped like bagpipes, and sometimes so long as to reach to the ground. They could be slashed at the sides to display the shirt beneath; they could be slit in two places, so that the hand could emerge from either opening. They were padded at the shoulders with wadding to make the chest look broad. Though forbidden by a law of Edward IV, to any yeoman or person under that degree, they continued to be worn by all who could afford them.

The shortness of the garments worn by young men made it necessary to wear joined hose, like modern tights. They were kept up by 'trussing the points', that is, by passing strings tipped with metal, like a modern bootlace, through eyelet holes in the lower edge of the doublet and the upper edge of the hose. Hose could be merely footed, in which case boots or shoes were necessary, or soled, pattens being added in wet weather. Hose were sometimes lined with leather.

A characteristic head-gear of the middle years of the century was the chaperon. This was chiefly worn by older men and was a development from the head-turban. It consisted

38

Male Costume, 1437. *From the brass in Kingston-on-Thames Church.*

of a roundlet, a wheel-shaped roll stuffed with silk or cotton, and a gorget consisting of folds of material usually cut in fancy shapes. This was sometimes worn not on the head but on the shoulder, and in this position it became a badge of livery, gradually decreasing in size. Centuries later, shrunk to minute dimensions, it was the cockade on a coachman's hat.

Hats became increasingly common as the fifteenth century progressed. They were of many varieties: a kind of top-hat with the crown shaped like an hour-glass, a bag-shaped hat with a rolled brim, a large hat with a balloon-shaped crown, a tall cone-shaped hat, and a brimless hat rather like a round-topped Turkish fez, from which it was probably derived, as the colour was almost always red. In the second half of the century appeared a pork-pie hat, with a close turned up brim and a jewelled ornament, and a wide hat often worn with a feather.

Women continued to wear the kirtle, the *cote-hardie*, the sideless surcoat and the *houppelande*, all of which have been already described. The kirtle, however, became less and less visible owing to the elaboration of the *houppelande*, now called the gown. The bodice of this was made to fit more closely with a low-cut front, baring the neck. The waist which was rather high, was confined by a narrow girdle and from it the skirt fell in loose folds to the ground. Long trains were quite usual. The sleeves were immense and often edged with fur. The sideless surcoat gradually fell out of use except as a ceremonial garment. The mantle grew increasingly rich, especially for ceremonial occasions. We read for example, in a contemporary manuscript, of 'a mantle of white cloth of gold damask, furred with ermine and fastened at the breast with a large cord curiously wrought with gold and silk tassels'.

The short and troubled reign of Richard III gave little opportunity for the development of fashion. There was, however, one striking change in ladies head-dresses: the transition from the butterfly veil to a kind of cloth hood, folded back from the face and falling in folds to the shoulders. When this was stiffened by a diamond-shaped structure framing the face it became the Tudor head-dress. Its shape can be seen very plainly in the portrait (now in the National Portrait Gallery in London) of Margaret, Countess of Richmond and mother of Henry VII. Old ladies wore, in addition, a linen gorget concealing the throat and falling down to the breast. This gave them the appearance of nuns, and indeed it was no rare thing for noble ladies to end their lives as abbesses. The costume of some modern orders of nuns is in fact very similar to the widow's dress of the closing years of the fifteenth century.

Men's dress after 1485 shows some changes, especially in the shape of footwear. The sharp-pointed shoes of the previous age became somewhat blunted in 1480 and ten years later shoes had gone to the opposite extreme, assuming the shape of a duck's bill. They were to become even broader under Henry VIII, but so long as his father was still on the throne, men's costume retained a certain medieval flavour. Henry VII and his courtiers, unlike their predecessors and successors, wore their hair long. Henry VII himself was economical and plain in his garb and not the kind of man who would have been likely to inaugurate or encourage new styles.

The Middle Ages

39

40

Male Costume, 1509. *From the brass in Great Cressington Church, Norfolk.*

CHAPTER FIVE

Tudor Costume

In the sixteenth century we begin to see, even in remote England, the influence of various forces which historians sum up under the word Renaissance. All over Europe the Middle Ages were coming to an end and new influences were at work everywhere. The day of the heavily armoured knight was over: as the century progresses we can watch armour falling gradually into disuse, although it was still worn on ceremonial occasions. National monarchies were beginning to arise, and one might have expected that this would have caused an increasing emphasis on national costumes. Actually, owing to the increased ease of communication, something was emerging which might well be called a European costume, as opposed to national costumes. In the writings of the period we hear constant complaints that Germans, Italians and Frenchmen were abandoning their own fashions to ape foreign modes.

In England the clothes worn by Henry VII and his Court were still medieval, although touched by Italian influences, but with the accession of Henry VIII all this was changed. Henry VIII was as extravagant as his father had been economical and not only were his clothes made of rich materials but they were also very different in shape. Costume, at this time, seems to have been designed to make a man look as wide as possible. The sleeves, which were often detachable so that they could be worn with different tunics, were pouched, padded and almost always slashed. Slashing, which consisted of cutting slits in the material and drawing the under-material through, is thought to have originated in Switzerland after the defeat of Charles the Bold by the Swiss mercenaries. The coloured silk tents of the Duke of Burgundy fell as plunder to the Swiss soldiers who cut them up to repair their own ragged garments and returned home in triumph. From the Swiss, the custom passed to the German mercenaries, thence to the French Court, and ultimately, in a modified form to England—close contact between France and England having been established in

41

1514 when Henry VII's sister Mary married Louis XII of France. The French and English nobles on this occasion competed with one another in gorgeousness of colour as they were to do half a dozen years later at the ceremonial meeting between the two kings which is known as the Field of the Cloth of Gold.

The general appearance of Henry VIII is well known to us from Holbein's famous picture. His costume consisted of a series of sleeveless garments, worn one over the other. Next to the body was a shirt, with a very low neck, and over this was worn a doublet with long skirts. This doublet was cut out at the top like a woman's bodice and the gap was filled in with a stomacher of richly patterned material. Over this was worn a kind of sleeveless overcoat, which had previously been long but by this time was being worn knee-length. (These coats were sometimes edged with fur.) The legs were clothed in hose which was a precursor of the later division into stockings and breeches as separate garments. The breeches were slashed and pouched like the sleeves, and were attached to the doublet by means of laces with metal tags known as points. The shoes, in contrast to the pointed shoes of the late medieval period, were extremely broad in the toe; these too were often slashed.

Hats were worn both indoors and out. There was a small round cap with flexible brim at the back and sides which could be turned down over the ears; a so-called Milan beret, with soft crown and broad brim, slit on either side and turned up and fastened with a metal tag; another cap rather like a modern one but with the brim all the way round, and a small bonnet with halo brim bordered with feathers. The last was the one worn by Henry VII as seen in nearly all his portraits. Hair was short and it was the fashion to wear a full beard.

Women's clothes were as pouched and slashed as those of the men. Skirts were shorter than those of the previous reign, but ampler and more richly embroidered. The chief garment was the kirtle which was a bodice and skirt sewn together. Over this was worn the gown, which was tight-fitting to the waist and then fell in ample folds, sometimes trailing on the ground. Both gown and kirtle had a low and square-cut neckline, under which could be seen the top of the chemise. At first the sleeves of the kirtle were tight fitting and could be seen at the wrists beneath the slightly wider sleeve of the gown. Gradually both grew larger until the outer sleeve became very large indeed and was occasionally worn with a deep turn back of fur. This sleeve can be seen very plainly in Holbein's portraits of Mary and Elizabeth as princesses and also in his portrait of the last wife of Henry VIII, Catherine Parr.

Women's head-dresses show an interesting development. Soon after the accession of Henry VII the butterfly head-dress with its wings of gauze spread out on wires was replaced by a kind of hood. In the centre of this was a stiffened kind of frame, giving the typical Tudor arch head-dress already described, so characteristic of the early years of Henry VIII's reign. Gradually the rigid frame slipped back until it was no more than a half-circle worn almost on the crown of the head. This was known as the French hood and it was fashionable for some years. We can see it in the early portraits of Mary, Queen of Scots.

The materials from which women's clothes were made at this period were extremely

43

Female Costume, 1528. *From the brass in Eton College Chapel, Bucks.*

German Noble, *c.* **1530.**
From the painting by Schef-
felin. (After Jacquemin.)

44

rich. Contemporary writers speak of cloth of gold, cloth of silver, silver embroidery, figured velvet and 'satin pinselled and overcast with golden threads'. There were gowns of taffeta enriched with the furs of lynxes, weasels, wolves and sables. Much jewellery was worn in the form of rings, bracelets and neck-chains. Stockings were dyed scarlet or purple and were sometimes embroidered and often slashed. Shoes (to quote Rabelais) 'were either of red, violet or crimson velvet, pinked and jagged'.

Towards the end of Henry VIII's reign, clothes both for men and women became less gorgeous, and the German influences we have noted, gradually faded away. Colours were not so bright and the excessive use of slashing was discontinued. His successor, Edward VI, had but a short reign and, as a mere youth, his influence on fashion was not likely to be considerable. Also he was surrounded by Puritan advisers and the fashions of his Court were marked by a quiet simplicity. The clothes of Francis I had been very similar to those of his contemporary Henry VIII, but his successor Henry II preferred not to wear garments made of silk and velvet or trimmed with gold and silver. He had a marked preference for black, as one can see quite plainly in his portrait by Clouet. Black and other sombre colours are supposed to have been copied from those of the Court of Spain, and indeed the Spanish influence is as marked in the second half of the sixteenth century as the German influence had been in the first. In England these influences were reinforced by the marriage of Mary Tudor to Philip of Spain, although at first the dress of those who came to London in 1554 in the train of the Spanish king had looked strange to English eyes. Instead of the sleeveless overcoat they wore a short cloak without sleeves or arm-holes and with a high turned-up collar. Their hats too were different. Instead of the flat cap with a brim all the way round, the Spaniards wore a hard hat with a high crown. The doublet, which was no longer slashed or pierced, fitted more closely to the body and the shoe was pointed instead of being broad-toed. The Spanish also wore long boots of Cordova leather ending above the knee, and we see already the outline of what we know as Elizabethan costume.

The accession of Elizabeth I put an end to the Spanish alliance, but the strange thing is that Spanish modes continued to dominate English fashion even when the two countries were at war. One evidence of this influence is seen in the ruff. Perhaps nothing is more typical of Spanish formality than this article. It was evolved from the frill at the top of the shirt collar, but by about 1570 it had increased to such a size that it became a separate article of attire. Ruffs were of various kinds, at first a single layer and later two, three or even more layers of gathered linen. They were kept in place by means of setting-sticks made of bone, ivory or wood. Starch for stiffening ruffs was introduced into England from Flanders in the 1560s. It was usually white but occasionally coloured red, blue or yellow. The usual material was linen but ruffs were sometimes made of lace or adorned with black or coloured silk embroidery.

When the ruff became very large it had to be supported by a wire frame known as an under-propper or *supportasse*, or by a *pickadil* which was an upright stiffened frame fixed at the back of the neck. It is plain that ruffs were status symbols, as obviously they could not be worn by anyone engaged in manual toil.

In Mary's reign women did not in general wear ruffs; they had instead a white collar

45

open in front and standing up stiffly at the back. The feminine ruff took some time to establish itself and did not last nearly so long as the male ruff, except in the modified form probably introduced by Marguerite of Navarre and adopted by Queen Elizabeth. This innovation consisted of splitting the ruff in front so to enable it to be worn with a *décolleté* gown. The curious winged effect thus achieved is familiar to us in nearly all portraits of Elizabeth.

Spanish influences are also shown in the introduction of the farthingale. This was a device for expanding women's skirts sometimes to extraordinary dimensions. In its earliest form it was known as the Spanish farthingale and consisted of an underskirt suspended by means of hoops growing wider towards the hem. This was a curious anticipation of the crinoline of the mid-nineteenth century. The new farthingale, or French farthingale, worn at Court in the 1560s and by almost every woman after 1580, was shaped like a drum. The skirt was draped horizontally over this and then fell vertically to the ground. The roll farthingale consisted of a padded bolster worn round the hips.

The principal male garment was still the doublet. It was now close-fitting, with a tight waist, pointed in front. Skirts had disappeared altogether or had shrunk to a mere narrow scalloped border immediately below the waist. Over this old men wore a gown which sometimes reached to the knee and sometimes to the ankle. The garment was also worn on ceremonial occasions or at home for warmth and comfort. This was the article of clothing worn by Malvolio in *Twelfth Night* and called a night-gown by Shakespeare: it was not, of course, a night-gown in our modern sense of the word. The materials used were velvet, satin or plain cloth; it was ornamented with braid and very often bordered and lined with fur. Another familiar article of clothing was the cloak, worn by nearly all men out of doors as well as in the house. It was a sign of social inferiority not to wear one. Usually it only reached to the waist but there was also a long cloak for travelling, which reached to the ankles.

Trunk hose are familiar to everyone from their frequent appearance in Elizabethan plays. Scholars distinguish two main styles: the first, which was more usual up to about 1570, was round like a pumpkin; the second style, which lasted from about 1570 to the early years of the seventeenth century, sloped out from the waist to a maximum swelling at mid-thigh. Both styles were frequently divided vertically into panes, or panels, with a lining of contrasting colour visible in the gaps between. From 1570 *cannions* were frequently worn. These had the appearance of another pair of breeches underneath the trunk hose, extending downwards to the knees and often in a contrasting colour or pattern. The stockings were often drawn over them, but sometimes the *cannions* were made wider and then fastened over the stockings below the knee, rather like modern knickerbockers.

In the 1580s a curious garment called a *mandilion* was much worn. It was a kind of loose, short jacket with hanging sleeves, and sometimes these sleeves were sham, like the sleeves of the modern academic gown. The top buttons only were fastened and the garment was then put on over the head; sometimes it was worn sideways with one sleeve hanging down the front and one behind. It was then said to be worn Collie-Weston wise, meaning crooked or awry.

A curious feature of this period was the universal use of bombast for the stuffing out

German Noble, *c.* **1530.** *From the painting by Scheffelin. (After Jacquemin.)*

47

48

Female Costume, 1557. *From the brass in Thornton Church, Bucks.*

of breeches. Bombast might be either of horse-hair, flock, wool, rags, flax or cotton. Bombasting indeed was so far almost all the use that had been found for cotton and an Elizabethan Herbal published towards the end of the century gave the cotton plant praise for 'bombastry'. Bran, although light, was not a very satisfactory material, for the story is told of an Elizabethan courtier who had a hole in his breeches from which the bran ran out in a steady stream as he bowed before the Queen. The bombasting of trunk hose reached its maximum between 1560 and 1570 while the waists grew ever tighter as if to emphasize the swelling of the thighs. There was bombast also in the peascod doublet, a Dutch fashion popular in England from 1575 to the end of the century. The padding produced a bulge which overhung the girdle and sometimes curved down to the fork. It has been preserved up to our own day in the traditional costume of Punch.

There was considerable variety in head-gear. The most common form was the flat cap with a brim all round. By an Act of Parliament of 1571 it was made compulsory for 'all above the age of six years, except the nobility and other persons of degree' to wear this cap, which, it was further ordained should be made of wool grown and manufactured in England. However, this law, like others of its kind, was frequently evaded and was repealed in 1597. There was also a bonnet with a very full, bag-like crown stiffened with buckram and sometimes worn with a feather. The hats included the *copotain* or 'sugar-loaf' hat, which had a high conical crown with a rather narrow brim, slightly turned up and rolled each side, thus causing it to resemble a modern bowler. Hats with a somewhat larger brim and a high, flat-topped crown looked forward to the top-hat of later ages. Many hats were decorated with feathers—ostrich feathers being very fashionable after about 1585; and the hats of all fine gentlemen had jewels to keep the feather in place or to decorate the hatband. Men's hair had been worn short in fashionable circles from 1535 and after 1560 all men were fairly closely cropped. Beards were almost universal and could be long and pointed, short and pointed, square or spade-shaped. The moustache was never worn alone.

Women's clothes show considerable variations from those worn in the first half of the century. The term kirtle was now only applied to the skirt, the bodice being a separate garment. Sometimes it was referred to as 'a pair of bodices' since it was made in two parts like a corset and stiffened with wood or whale-bone rods known as busks, inserted into sheaths in the lining. The bodice was tight-fitting, ending as a point at the waist. The neck could be either low or high; when high it had either a standing collar left open at the throat or a small Medici collar. The sleeves, up to 1560, were funnel-shape with a broad turn-back cuff ending at the elbow. For the rest of the century they were usually close-fitting to the wrist, sometimes slashed and puffed and finished with a little ruff. From about 1580 onwards the bodice was divided down the middle and the space filled in with a stomacher. This was made of rich material often matching the sleeves but different from the bodice and sometimes elaborately embroidered or studded with jewels. It was often stiffened with pasteboard or canvas. Coming to a sharp point at or even below the waist it gives us the long-bodied effect of women in Elizabethan portraits. Women's sleeves at this time could be bombasted like the trunk hose of men. What were called demi-cannon sleeves worn in the closing years of the century were distended with buckram, wire or whale-bone set in the lining.

49

Italian Princess, *c.* **1580.** (*After Jacquemin.*)

Women, like men, sometimes wore a gown over the bodice and skirt on ceremonial occasions and for warmth at home. Such garments must have been very necessary in winter in the long galleries of Elizabethan houses. For travelling on horseback—even women at this period usually travelled in this fashion—a cloak was worn as well as an extra skirt which protected the kirtle from the dirt and dust of the road and was known as a safeguard. Throughout the Elizabethan period women's hair showed an increasing tendency to more elaborate dressing. The back hair was usually plaited or piled behind the head and generally hidden by the head-dress, but the front hair left the forehead uncovered and was arranged in various styles. Until 1575 women usually wore it divided by a centre parting and bunched out at the temples. In the 70s it began to be worn turned back over a pad and later, the centre parting was given up and the hair was raised over a wired support called a palisadoe. Sometimes the same effect was obtained by means of pads. The hair was frequently dyed and false hair and even wigs were worn. The hair ornament known as a *billiment* was a band of silk, velvet or satin garnished with jewels. Sometimes, especially for brides, it was made entirely of gold, and could cost as much as sixteen guineas, a considerable sum for those days.

Women were allowed considerably more variety in the choice of head-gear. The French hood, which we have already described, continued into the next century but was now worn only by unfashionable women. There was an increasing use of hats and bonnets for riding or travelling. They were like those worn by men but were usually smaller. The *pipkin*, sometimes worn over a hair net, was a small, flat bonnet perched on the top of the head and often ornamented with a plume and a jewelled headband. A similar cap, but with a high crown, was much worn in the 1570s. Hats had tall crowns and were trimmed with velvet, silk or *crêpe*. There was also a low-crowned hat resembling a bowler, and country women wore wide-brimmed hats made of straw. Another and rather curious article of head-gear was known as the arched hood, which was worn especially at funerals. This was made of heavy material, one border threaded with wire and curved to make what looked like an arch over the head. The side supports were fixed to the shoulder so that the women wearing the arched hood appeared to be standing in a kind of sentry box. Most women wore a caul or coif but even this was not always considered necessary, especially for girls and young women. A Dutch traveller who visited England in the 1570s remarked: 'Married women only wear a hat both in the street and in the house; those unmarried go without a hat although ladies of distinction have lately learnt to cover their faces with silken masks or vizards.' These masks were worn in public to avoid recognition or as a protection of the complexion against the weather. They were usually oval in shape with holes for the eyes and could be made of velvet, silk or taffeta and lined with thin leather or silk. Sometimes they had a button inside which could be gripped by the teeth to hold the mask in position.

An interesting feature of fashion at this period is the introduction of knitting. Knitwear, especially knitted caps and gloves, was worn by the nobility at the end of the fifteenth century but knitting did not become really established in England until the second half of the sixteenth. Knitted stockings began to replace those made of cloth, and as they were much better fitting they were eagerly welcomed. The Earl of Oxford is said to have

52

Female Costume, 1589. *From the brass in Hascombe Church, Devon.*

bought a pair of knitted silk stockings from France as a present for Queen Elizabeth. The stockings were coloured crimson or blue and sometimes clocked with silver or gold thread. Thicker stockings were often worn underneath for warmth. As suspenders had not yet been invented, it was necessary to keep the stockings in place by means of garters. These were tied below the knee and could be made of silk and embroidered with silk or metallic thread.

Among the aristocracy gloves were much worn by both men and women. Sometimes these ended at the wrist, but the typical Elizabethan glove is of the gauntlet variety with the gauntlets richly embroidered. The fingers were often slashed to make room for the rings. At first gloves of all kinds were imported from France and Spain but from 1580 onwards they were manufactured in England. Perfumed gloves were much prized and it was the fashion to give them away at weddings.

Handkerchiefs trimmed with lace and sometimes even embroidered and fringed were carried by both men and women. Suspended from her girdle by a ribbon or chain, the fashionable woman also carried a purse, muff, fan, mirror or pomander, or any combination of these. The fan was not of the folding variety but usually consisted of a plume of feathers attached to a handle which sometimes had a small mirror let into the base. The muffs were small and tubular.

Much jewellery was worn by both men and women; in fact, some of Elizabeth's courtiers are said to have carried a fortune on their backs. Jewels were not only used as lockets, pendants, bracelets, pomanders, rings and ear-rings, but were also sewn on to the garments themselves. The stomachers of Queen Elizabeth literally blazed with gems. But splendid as the late Tudor costume was, one has to admit that, at least as far as women were concerned, it showed a marked decline in both comfort and grace from the clothes worn in the first half of the sixteenth century. It was too rigid, too stiff, too formal and with its long pointed stomacher and farthingale almost completely deformed the shape of the female figure. The clothes depicted in the Holbein portraits have an ease and elegance which was not to be recaptured until the dynasty of the Tudors was extinct.

54

Frances, Duchess of Richmond and Lennox. *Engraving by W. van de Passe, 1623.*

CHAPTER SIX

The Seventeenth Century

Centuries are arbitrary divisions and the events of history and of costume history do not fall neatly into periods of a hundred years. The old Queen Elizabeth lived until 1603 and even after her death there was no drastic change in fashion. Anne of Denmark, the Consort of James I, wore the farthingale and the pointed stiff stomacher kept in place by means of the rigid busks. Her hair was dressed high above the forehead and turned back over a roll. So far as women were concerned these Elizabethan fashions continued until about 1625. The men showed a little more tendency to experiment, notably in the form of their breeches, the favourite kinds in the early years of the century being known as venetians and galligas-kins. Venetians were wide and sometimes bombasted round the hips but were narrower over the thighs and shaped to button or tie below the knee. Galligaskins were closer fitting but were otherwise very similar. A third variety known as slops were very wide, baggy breeches fastened below the knee. They were sometimes known as Dutch slops.

The dates of French history are sometimes more convenient for our purpose than those of English history. Henry IV of France was assassinated in 1610 and the accession of Louis XIII did mark a real change, not in the general outline of clothes, but in the shape of neck-wear. The ordinary ruff which had been universally worn in the early years of the century gave way to what was known as the falling ruff. It was similar in construction to the ordinary ruff but sloped down to the shoulders from a high neck-band to which it was sewn. Both these forms could be replaced by the standing band which was a semicircular collar edged with lace, round at the back and high in the neck, and with the straight front edges tied under the chin with a string. It could be starched or kept in position by means of an underpropper, attached to the neck of the doublet behind. An innovation which pointed to the future was the falling band, a wide collar falling upon the shoulders. This is the typical Van Dyke collar known to us in such paintings as the Laughing Cavalier. It

55

was usually edged with lace, and a passion for lace is the characteristic mark of the seventeenth century. Lace was also worn at the wrists in the form of a hand ruff (later called a ruffle) which echoed the form and decoration of the ruff round the neck. Lace, strangely enough, was also worn in the tops of boots.

Footwear began to exhibit some notable changes. Heels made of leather or wood became universal. About 1635 the toes of boots and shoes became square and remained so for the rest of the century. A notable feature from 1610 onwards was the shoe-rose, a kind of ribbon rosette which grew so large that it might sometimes cover the whole foot. The real innovation was in the shape of boots. The Elizabethans had worn their long boots of cordovan leather pulled up to mid-thigh. The subjects of James I, and still more those of Charles I, began to turn them down, sometimes as low as mid-calf. These with their wide tops are the characteristic footwear of Cavaliers. They were adorned with large and elaborate spurs, with star-shaped rowels. These were worn even when not riding.

Women's clothes showed very little change until the middle of the 1620s. The farthingale was abandoned and skirts changed their shape. They were bunched up in a kind of bustle, to reveal an under-petticoat often more decorative than the skirt itself. The bodice was short-waisted and the *décolletage* was now round instead of square. The effect of *décolletage* was, however, rather diminished by the general use of a kind of fichu of lace or lawn worn over the shoulders. The rigid Elizabethan stomacher was replaced by a more flexible front called a *piece*, but sometimes the bodice was merely laced up the front with a ribbon. The sleeves were leg-of-mutton shaped and often paned and puffed.

There was also an easier type of bodice, close-fitting and flaring from the waist, known as a jacket or waistcoat.

The gown was a loose garment fitting the shoulders and hanging in spreading folds to the ground. After about 1630 it often had a fitted bodice joined to a full-gathered skirt. The night-gown was a *négligé* worn for comfort at home. Towards 1640 it began to have short sleeves. It resembled what we should call a house-coat.

Women's neck-wear echoed masculine fashions. Women wore the closed ruff until about 1620 but, after about 1615, it began to slope downwards and settled on the shoulders in the 1630s, when it was known, as we have noted, as the falling collar. In Holland, as we can see from the paintings of Rembrandt and Franz Hals, the Elizabethan ruff, sometimes grown to gigantic proportions, lasted until the middle of the century. Strangely enough, in their passion for fine linen, women sometimes wore the ruff and falling collar together. The collar, as with men, was often edged with rich lace. In France the excessive use of lace led, in 1633, to a law prohibiting this and other kinds of finery; but like all such law, it remained ineffective. In England it was the Puritans who tried to set an example of more sober attire. They wore the falling collar without lace, and their clothes in general bore a close resemblance to those of their Dutch contemporaries. The Cavaliers, on the other hand, were much affected by French modes, and permitted themselves brighter colours and more costly materials.

As is well known, the most obvious difference between the Puritans and the Cavaliers in England at the beginning of the Civil War was in their style of hairdressing. The Cavaliers

57

French Nobleman. *Engraving by A. Bosse, c. 1625.*

58

English Lady. *Engraving by R. Gaywood after W. Hollar, 1654.*

wore their hair long, falling in ringlets to the shoulders. The Puritans wore their hair short and so were known as Crop-ears or Roundheads.

There were at this period considerable changes in the shape of hats. The typical Cavalier hat was a low-crowned hat with a wide flexible brim adorned with a feather. Charles I however wore what we usually think of as the Puritan hat. This was a tall hat with a stiff crown but its brim was much wider than that of the top-hat of later ages. Sometimes the soft, wide-brimmed hat was cocked at one side. Hats were made of felt, velvet—stiffened with buckram—and beaver, the last item being the most expensive. The lining of hats was usually of velvet or taffeta. Women's hats were similar to those of the men, but sometimes instead of a hat they wore what was known as a head-rail. This was a large square of material with one corner turned back. It was pinned round the back of the head and could be long enough to reach to the ground. Instead of this could be worn a gauze veil draped over the head and face. When a hat was worn, a coif (a close-fitting hood shaped like a baby's bonnet) was frequently worn under it.

The Restoration of Charles II in 1660 caused many of the latest French fashions to be imported into England, the courtiers of Whitehall vying with those of Versailles in extravagant attire. For half a dozen years the strangest fashions prevailed. Men's doublets were so short that there was a gap between them and the breeches, through which the shirt could be seen. The sleeves also were extremely short, revealing much of the white sleeves of the shirt; but the strangest feature was the shape of the breeches themselves. They were called petticoat breeches, or Rhinegraves, and were so immensely wide that they resembled divided skirts. Indeed, they were so ample that, as Pepys tells us in his *Diary* for 1661, it was possible to put both legs into one of the compartments without noticing it. Except for neck-wear, lace was for a time abandoned, its place being taken by ribbons. These were attached to the waist, to the skirts and even to the knees, and immense quantities were used. We hear of 'a suit and cloak of satin, trimmed with thirty-six yards of silver ribbon'; there is a specimen of petticoat breeches in the Victoria and Albert Museum trimmed with no less than 250 yards of ribbon in bunches. Such extravagances were, of course, only to be found at Court. Ordinary men still went about in the closed breeches of the previous generation. The falling band about the neck had now shrunk to a kind of bib. It was decorated, in fashionable circles, with a broad border of lace. Hair was worn long, falling about the shoulders.

Women's clothes showed less striking changes during the first few years after the Restoration. However, the close-fitting and boned bodice had again become long-waisted, sloping to a deep point in front. There was a deep horizontal *décolleté*, either leaving the shoulders bare, or covering them with a broad lace *bertha* or a diaphanous scarf. The sleeves were full to the elbow and rather short, allowing the full sleeve of the *chemise* to emerge. The skirt, which was gathered in small pleats at the waist and hung in loose folds to the ground, was usually open in front, showing the petticoat underneath. This petticoat or underskirt was sometimes very ornamental and trimmed with several flounces of lace or frills. The hairstyle showed corkscrew curls massed on each side of the face. It was fashionable to go bareheaded both indoors and out, the large hats with tall crowns and broad brims being now only worn by the middle classes.

It is not often that we can give an exact date for a change in fashion, but the year 1666 marked a real revolution in masculine attire. Three diarists have recorded it in precise terms. Rugge in his *Diurnal* for October 11th, 1666, notes:

In this month his Majestie and whole Court changed the fashion of their clothes, viz., a coat of cloth pinkt, with a white taffety under the cutts. This in length reached the calf of the leg, and upon that a surcoate cutt at the breast which hung loose and shorter than the rest six inches. The breeches were Spanish cut, and buskins, some of cloth, some of leather, but of the same colour as the vest or garment, never the like fashion since William the Conqueror.

It is probable that Rugge knew extremely little of English costume 'since William the Conqueror'; but he was at least convinced that a very important change had taken place.

Samuel Pepys too describes the new costume and is even more careful of his dates. On October 8th, 1666, he notes in his *Diary*:

The King hath yesterday in Council declared his resolution of setting a fashion of clothes which he will never alter.

On October 15th, he comments:

This day the King begins to put on his vest, and I did see several persons of the House of Lords and Commons too, great courtiers who are in it; being a long cassocke close to the body, of black cloth, and pinked with white silke under it and a coat over it, and the legs ruffled with black riband like a pidgeon's leg; and, upon the whole, I wish the King may keep it, for it is a very fine and handsome garment.

Evelyn's *Diary* is equally informative. Under the date October 18th, 1666, he remarks:

To Court, it being the first time his Majesty put himself solemnly into the Eastern fashion of vest, changing doublet, stiff collar, bands and cloak into the comely dress after the Persian mode, with girdles or straps and shoe strings and garters in the buckles, of which some were set with precious stones, resolving never to alter it, and to leave the French mode, which had hitherto obtained to our great expense and reproach. Upon which divers Courtiers and gentlemen gave his Majesty gold by way of wager that he would not persist in this resolution.

There is a slight discrepancy in the dates and it would seem that Pepys is the more accurate for he makes a further comment in the entry in his *Diary* for October 17th:

The Court is all full of vests, only my Lord of St. Albans not pinked, but plain black; and they say the King says that pinking upon white makes them look too much like magpies and therefore has bespoke one of plain velvet.

The interesting thing is that Evelyn should have described the new garment as 'the Eastern fashion of vest' and as a 'dress after the Persian mode'. That it was considered to be of Oriental origin is shown by a passage in a work entitled: *England's vanity: or the voice of God against the sin of Pride in Dress and Apparel*, which appeared in 1683 and which states that the new fashion was popularly called Turkish.

Certainly the garment introduced by Charles, with its tight-fitting body, its wide skirts and its buttons all the way down, bore a close resemblance to the Persian coat. The pockets in the skirts of the latter had vertical openings, but so had the earliest examples known of the English vest. But while the Persian sleeves were long, even covering part of the hand,

Man wearing Rhinegraves, *c.* 1665, and Man wearing the 'Persian' Dress, 1670. *Engravings by S. le Clerc.*

'Man of Quality'. *Engraving by J. de St. Jean, 1693.*

the English sleeves were short, in order to show as much as possible of the full shirt-sleeve, with its lace cuff.

Rugge mentions the breeches of Spanish cut, and these finally became universal, but the petticoat breeches were still sometimes worn with the new vest. Over the vest a loose overcoat was worn and this was originally intended only for outdoor wear. But in the end the overcoat became the coat and the vest, when it came to be cut shorter, became what was later called the waistcoat.

Charles II and his courtiers may have imagined that by adopting the new clothes they were breaking away from French fashions, but a very similar garment to the vest had been introduced at the Court of the French King, Louis XIV, as early as 1662. Its use was at first limited to a few privileged courtiers, but it soon made its influence felt on contemporary dress.

These garments were the ancestors of those we wear today, but when the mode of coat and waistcoat was first established, the waistcoat was almost as long as the over-garment and was as liberally garnished with buttons. These, however, were not fastened all the way down. The coat was at first rather plain, elaborate embroidery being reserved for the undergarment, and the wide falling collar disappeared, as the coat made it inconvenient. Instead, a cravat of lace or muslin was worn, sometimes tied with a bow. From this developed, in time, our modern neck-wear. The breeches were almost entirely concealed by the length of coat and waistcoat, and the frills of lace which had once descended below the knee completely disappeared.

All these changes were steps in the direction of simplicity; but at this stage a new element entered into male fashion which gives the closing years of the seventeenth century and the opening years of the eighteenth their most characteristic and artificial note. This was the invention of the periwig, perhaps the most extraordinary event that has ever happened in the history of male costume. The wig had, of course, been known long before. It was worn by the Ancient Egyptians. Queen Elizabeth wore a wig in her old age, and even Mary, Queen of Scots did not disdain the use of false hair. But now the periwig was not a mere addition to or substitute for natural hair but a definite article of clothing in its own right.

This time the mode undoubtedly came from France. The fashion for wearing the hair long had compelled many even under Louis XIII to have recourse to false locks, but the young Louis XIV was well provided with natural hair and even when he adopted the wig it had holes in it through which his own hair appeared. The very fact, however, that his courtiers wished to appear like him induced them to adopt a perruque, or periwig, and by an edict of 1673 Louis created no less than two hundred posts of perruquiers at Court. The fashion had by this time been established for nearly a decade.

Fortunately, thanks once again to Samuel Pepys, we know almost exactly when the new French periwigs began to be worn in England. In the entry in his *Diary* under November 2nd, 1663, he remarks: 'I heard the Duke [of York] say that he was going to wear a perriwigg; and they say the King also will. I never to this day observed that the King is mighty gray.'

Pepys hastened to adopt the new fashion, and six days later went to church in a wig for the first time. 'I found that my coming in a perriwigg did not prove so strange as I was afraid it would, for I thought that all the church would presently have cast their eyes all upon me.' But it was not until February 15th, 1664, that Royalty caught up with him: 'To White Hall to the Duke, where he first put on a perriwigg today: but methought his hair cut short in order thereto did look very pretty of itself, before he put on his periwigg.'

It was not until April 18th, that he was able to note: 'To Hide Parke, where I have not been since last year; where I saw the King with his periwigg but not altered at all.'

These are invaluable references, but Pepys puts us still further in his debt by giving some indication of the cost of buying and maintaining a wig, and also the dangers of wearing one in an age not notable for its cleanliness. On Sunday, September 3rd, 1665 (1665 was, of course, the year of the Great Plague of London), he notes:

Up and put on my coloured silk suit, very fine, and my new periwigg, bought a good while since, but durst not wear, because the plague was in Westminster when I bought it; and it is a wonder what will be the fashion after the plague is done, as to periwiggs, for nobody will dare to buy any haire for fear of the infection, that it had been cut off the heads of people dead of the plague.

The Great Plague had, however, no effect whatever on the wearing of false hair, for some nine months later Pepys found even ladies in wigs, worn as part of riding costume:

Walking in the galleries at White Hall, I found the Ladies of Honour dressed in their riding garb, with boots and doublets with deep skirts, just for the all the world like mine, and buttoned their doublets up the breast, with perriwiggs and with hats.

With regard to the cost of wearing a wig two entries must suffice:

March 29th [1667]. To a Periwigg-maker's, and there bought two periwiggs, mighty fine indeed; too fine, I thought, for me: but he persuaded me, and I did buy them for four pounds ten shillings the two.

May 30th [1668]. Up, and put on a new, summer black bombazin suit; and being come now to an agreement with my barber to keep my perriwig in good order at 20 shillings a year, I am like to go very spruce, more than I used to do.

Both the amounts mentioned represented a considerable charge on seventeenth century incomes; but the prices paid by Pepys were very moderate compared with those paid by the fops, and by members of the aristocracy.

The full-bottomed wig undoubtedly gave great dignity to the countenance, but it must have been both hot and uncomfortable for general use, and in any active exertion extremely difficult to keep on the head. In the battles of the end of the seventeenth century it is recorded that the field after the conflict was strewn with the hats and periwigs of the officers who had lost both in the fury of the charge. The hats too were very large and they had assumed by this time the shape and fashion they were to retain for more than a century. The hat worn plain by the Roundheads and adorned with a feather by the Cavaliers was distinguished by its high crown and its wide brim. Charles II brought in the so-called French hat, with wide brim and shallow crown, adorned with even more feathers. At the funeral of General Monk in 1670, hats were very small in the brim also. Finally, the crown settled down to a moderate height and the brim, which had become wider again, underwent the process known as cocking, which meant that one portion of it was turned up either at the front, back, or on one side of the head.

'Woman of Quality'. *Engraving by J. de St. Jean, 1694.*

At first this seems to have been a matter of individual fancy (we hear, for instance, of the Monmouth Cock) but in the reign of William and Mary the hat began to be turned up in three places, thus forming the three-cornered hat which became the only possible head-gear for a gentleman throughout the civilized world. The lower orders continued to wear their hats uncocked.

In women's clothes, in the last quarter of the seventeenth century, there was no change comparable with the real revolution in male attire. The long pointed waists continued and gradually became tighter. The tucked-up skirts grew more and more formal in appearance, the general outline of the figure stiffer and narrower. The large collar of lace went out of fashion in the early 70s, although out of doors a kerchief called a palatine covered the bare shoulders. In the 1690s the characteristic feature of female dress was the top-knot called in France, the country of its origin, a *fontange* after one of the favourites of Louis XIV who, the story goes, finding her hair disarranged while hunting, tied it up hastily with one of her garters. The King expressed his admiration, and the mode was launched; next day all the Court ladies appeared with their hair tied with a ribbon with a bow in front. The fashion quickly crossed the Channel and is one of the earliest examples of a French mode imposing itself on England, universally and almost at once.

Soon a simple bow of ribbon was not enough. Lace was added, and then a cap was added to the lace, with a wire frame to support the ever increasing height of the structure. It was then called, perhaps in irony, a *commode* and in England was known also as a tower. In the *Ladies' Dictionary* of 1694 it was described as 'a frame of wire two or three stories high, fitted to the head, and covered with tiffany or other thin silk, being now compleated into the whole headdress.' Moralists, as usual, regarded the new fashion with grave misgiving and duly denounced it in their sermons.

CHAPTER SEVEN

The Eighteenth Century

Louis XIV continued to rule France until his death in 1715, but the closing years of his reign were marked by a series of French defeats. The natural discouragement which resulted and the formal piety of Madame de Maintenon had a dampening effect on the evolution of new fashions. A similar situation existed in England. When Queen Anne succeeded to the throne at the beginning of the century she was already middle-aged and ailing and had neither the ambition nor the originality of mind to inaugurate new modes. What influence she had was conservative, especially so far as the formal dress of men was concerned; she was once highly offended when Lord Bolingbroke, summoned in haste, presented himself before her in a *ramillie*, or tie-wig, instead of one of the fullbottomed variety.

Women's clothes maintained the stiff decorum of the previous reign. The lace cap was still worn but had now lost its extravagant height. There was a fairly deep square *décolletage*, with a tight corsage visibly laced in front; the slit skirt was bunched back to give the effect of a bustle and to reveal the flounced and embroidered petticoat, usually partially concealed by an apron. The sleeves had wide turn-backs like those of the men, but higher up the arm, with a lace ruffle visible below.

The exception to this formality was the dress known as the *sac* or sack. It was undoubtedly of French origin and Pepys speaks of it as early as 1668 when he records: 'My wife this day put on first her French gown called a Sac, which became her very well.' However, no other mention of a *sac* at this period is known, and it is possible that it was of a different form from the *sac* worn in the reign of Queen Anne.

The sack was a comparatively simple and easy gown, with the characteristic of a long, broad fold hanging from the neck down the back. It is frequently called the Watteau gown from the frequency with which dresses of this kind appear in his pictures. It could be

67

Viscount Cobham. *Engraving by J. Faber after G. Kneller, 1730.*

of different forms, varying from a loose dressing-gown shape with vast hanging sleeves and many folds, to a shape clinging closely to the bust and falling gracefully down into ever-widening skirts and having short tight sleeves. The flowing robe entirely hid the whole underdress from the throat to the slippers; in fact nothing could be seen but a small portion of the corset adorned with a row of ribbons. Watteau did not come to England until 1719 when Queen Anne was dead, but the so-called Watteau gown had been growing in favour for some years.

The most striking change in women's dress at this period was due to the reintroduction of hoops. These had vanished from female costume in England when the Elizabethan farthingale fell out of fashion. They had however been preserved in the conservative courts of Spain and Portugal and when Catherine of Braganza came to England to marry Charles II her distended skirt provoked only ridicule. But distended skirts were seen again in England about the year 1710. They were known as hooped skirts, the hoops being of whalebone or osier-rods held together by ribbons. The structure bore some resemblance to a basket, and the French word for basket, *panier*, was applied to this method of distending the skirt. The paniered skirt assumed its characteristic form about 1730. Unlike the earlier farthingale or the later crinoline, it did not distend the skirt all the way round but only at the sides. It could sometimes be as wide as eighteen feet.

The essential lines of men's dress (coat, vest and breeches) had become fixed at the beginning of the eighteenth century and remained almost unchanged for a couple of generations. Coats and waistcoats reached almost to the knees with large pockets in the skirts of each. The skirts themselves were sometimes reinforced with linen, buckram or whalebone, and from the pleats protruded the hilt of the sword attached to a baldrick or belt worn underneath. The sleeves had enormous turned back cuffs. The stockings were gartered below the knee but drawn up over it and could be of coloured silk with gold or silver clocks. The falling collar, even in its narrow form, had now been replaced by the neckcloth or cravat which consisted of a strip of white material about a foot wide and a yard long, twisted round the neck and knotted in front. There was considerable variety in the manner of tying it, and each variety had a special name. A Steinkerk was a lace cravat tied very loosely, with the ends passed through a buttonhole in the coat. It was so called after the Battle of Steinkirk, where the French officers went into action so hurriedly that they had no time to tie their cravats properly; and the fashion was popular in England in spite of the fact that Steinkerk was an English defeat.

The most remarkable feature of men's dress at this period was the wig. This had now become universal among men with any pretensions to gentility. The natural hair was clipped and even shaved close and the structure of artificial curls imposed upon it. In its earliest and most elaborate form the full-bottomed wig was divided into three masses of curls, two in front of the shoulders and one hanging down the back. Above the forehead the hair rose into two peaks or horns, sometimes exaggerated to grotesque proportions, but this fashion did not last very long even among the leisured, owing to its inconvenience. When the curls were tied back the wig was known as a tie-wig. Another popular style, at first chiefly in use among soldiers, was the bag-wig, the hair at the back being enclosed in a bag of gummed black taffeta with a bow of the same material. The pigtail was almost as popular as the bag-wig and for the same reasons of convenience. The *toupet*, or hair immediately over the forehead, was often natural, the join between the wig and the real hair being disguised by a liberal use of powder. The strange fashion of sprinkling the hair with either white or grey powder lasted for the greater part of the eighteenth century. The three-cornered hat was now universal but grew gradually smaller as the century wore on.

The general cut of men's clothes began to be slightly modified about 1750. The front skirts of the coat were cut back exposing the front of the breeches. The side pleats with buttons moved towards the back and buckram and other stiffenings were no longer used. The skirts of waistcoats had been gradually shortened and by this time they reached just over the hips and were cut away in front at the waist. The turn-backs of the cuffs were much diminished in size. In contrast to the fashion at the beginning of the century the coat and waistcoat were now sometimes made of the same material and were much more elaborately patterned. Suits could be made of cut velvet or embroidered silk, the embroidery often involving months or even years of labour on the part of embroideresses, whose skill and taste have never been surpassed. There was much use of decorative buttons, these being made of metal, mother-of-pearl or enamel. Enamelled buttons with miniature pictures of dogs, foxes, stags and horses were very popular in the 50s and 60s. There was some change in the form of neck-wear, the Steinkirk and other cravats being gradually replaced by the stock which was a neck-cloth folded closely round the neck and buckled or tied behind. In spite of the fact that the stock buckle was generally concealed by the wig it was often costly and might be made of gold and silver; sometimes it was set with diamonds.

COSTUME

Wigs continued to be worn by all classes except for a brief period in the middle 60s when it was fashionable among younger men to wear their own hair. The Master Peruke Makers of London thereupon presented a petition to George III against this mode which threatened their trade with extinction. There were innumerable varieties of wigs. The full-bottomed wig was now only worn by legal and ecclesiastical dignitaries. The bob-wig which had several rows of curls at the side and back of the head could be worn either long or short. The scratch-bob was usually the colour of the natural hair. It only covered part of the head, the natural hair being brushed back from the forehead and blended with the wig by means of pomatum. There were also wigs with pigtails and from 1750 onwards these tended to be made smaller and with fewer curls. The bag-wig was still in fashion but was often worn with a rosette instead of a stiff bow at the back. Wigs were not always made of human hair; horse-hair, goat's hair, foxes' tails, mohair, worsted and even copper and iron wire were also used. It was quite a costly business keeping a wig in order. Anything from ten shillings to a guinea a week might be spent, which would be the equivalent, perhaps of £4 or £5 to-day.

When we see a production of an eighteenth century play, we see women wearing wigs as well as men. In reality this was not so. Women in general wore their own hair, but dressed to look as artificial as possible and almost always powdered. In the 1750s the hair was dressed close to the head: a very charming style which can be seen to its best advantage in portraits of Madame de Pompadour. In the early 60s the hair began to rise from the head. It was at first combed smoothly back from the forehead and temples and twisted

Sir Chaloner Ogle. *Engraving by J. Faber after C. Zinke, 1741.*

71

72

Gentleman in Walking Dress. *Engraving by L. Truchy after H. Gravelot, 1744.*

into a small bun at the top, but from about 1764 (and a little earlier in France) the front hair began to be raised on rolls of wool or horse-hair and frizzed, sometimes with the addition of false hair. By 1768 the front hair was dressed very high off the forehead, and in the 70s it rose to quite fantastic proportions: the *toupet* was built up over the forehead to a height often exceeding the length of the face. This necessitated the use of cushions or large pads stuffed with horse-hair or wool. Sometimes wire supports were used, the hair, with false hair added, being plastered with paste and pomatum and drawn up over the wire frame. The whole structure might be crowned with baskets of flowers, plates of fruit, and even with a ship in full sail. It was far from a comfortable mode. The *Ladies' Magazine* for March, 1776 notes:

I have seen several ladies, very handsome, so disguised and features quite distorted, by the horrid drag of their hair to a height absolutely half as tall as themselves, and so loaded with game, flowers, fruit, herbs, ribbons, pins, etc. . . . that it has really seemed a pain for them to move or speak for fear the wonderful building be demolished.

The dressing of the head for a fashionable function occupied three or four hours, and ladies going to Court had sometimes to get up in the middle of the night in order to be ready. The high head-dress was also a most insanitary fashion, as once it was erected it was impossible to comb and became a veritable breeding ground for lice. The little ivory claws at the end of a long stick sometimes seen in antiquarian shops and usually described as back-scratchers were really for the purpose of inserting in the high head-dress to relieve the intolerable itching caused by these pests. Sometimes the head-dress was so elaborate that no hat was necessary. When one was worn it was either very large, enclosing the whole head, or very small and perched forward like a decoration on the top of the hair. Naturally women wanted the latest information about hairstyles, and it is interesting to note that the fashion-plate which was just beginning to come into existence at this period was at first concerned with hairdressing rather than with clothes. A *Recueil de Coiffures* was published in Paris in 1778, it being taken for granted that in all such matters the French knew best. In the 1780s the hair of women, instead of being dressed very high, began to be dressed very broad, the *toupet* being frizzed or crimped so as to stand out round the face; or the hair could be dressed in loose ringlets all over the head. Red hair powder was fashionable in the early 80s, but the mode did not last long.

The general form of women's dress now began to be somewhat modified. By 1780 hoops had almost entirely disappeared, their place being taken by small pads or cushions fastened to the hips, and then by a single pad at the back, giving a kind of bustle effect. The materials of which dresses were made became less rich—figured silks and brocades giving place to dresses of plain muslin. This was due in part to the example of Queen Marie-Antoinette who liked to play at being a milkmaid, but it was in part an English fashion, English ladies spending much more of their time on their country estates than their French counterparts and preferring to wear what might be called country clothes. Some women adopted a semi-masculine riding costume, the bodice being made in imitation of a man's coat and waistcoat with overlapping *revers*, and the skirt full, simple and without trimmings. Even on town dresses, trimmings were abandoned in favour of ruches of muslin or lace, arranged in flounces and sewn to the edge of the dress.

Men's clothes showed a similar trend towards simplicity, embroidery being now confined almost entirely to the waistcoat. The front skirts of the coat were sometimes cut away in a square slice, like those of our modern full evening dress, enabling the wearer to sit a horse more easily. The three-cornered hat was often replaced by a round brimmed high-crowned one which is visibly the ancestor of the modern 'topper'. In a word, men were beginning to wear country clothes, and this is a revolution of such importance that it must be considered in some detail, especially since Frenchmen as well as Englishmen were affected by it.

There existed in France in the period just before the French Revolution, an extra-ordinary enthusiasm for all things English. French advanced thinkers found much to admire in English life: its liberty, its comparative lack of privilege, and, above all, its simplicity. The French costume, which had become the dress of every civilized man in the eighteenth century, was essentially a Court—or at least an urban—dress. But Englishmen had always had a passion for country life and so had modified the French Court costume to suit their own requirements. These modifications the French themselves now adopted. It was part of the revolt against the *Ancien Régime*. The cry was—'Back to Nature'.

The same impulse caused a considerable modification in the clothes worn by children. Until about the middle of the eighteenth century, children, in the upper classes at least, had been dressed as miniature replicas of their elders, even little boys being rigged out in silk stockings, satin breeches and embroidered coats. Little girls suffered even more for, from their tenderest years, their bodies were enclosed in boned corsets; sometimes they were compelled to sleep in them and it is small wonder that they often grew up languid and listless and even with curvature of the spine. The great French writer Jean-Jacques Rousseau was a strong opponent of all the artificialities of civilization. He was also much concerned with the education of children and was one of the first to insist that they were not inferior copies of grown-ups but creatures with lives of their own, with different problems and different needs. One of these needs is to be able to play and this is obviously impossible if children's clothes are tight, formal and easily dirtied. Gradually these ideas began to influence the way in which children were dressed and, towards the end of the eighteenth century, there was a real improvement. Girls were allowed to abandon the tight corsets, the hoops, the heavily embroidered skirts and the elaborate head-dresses, and were clad in simple garments, usually white, with a ribbon round the waist. The boys were given open-throated shirts, plain jackets and loose trousers—a curious anticipation of the grown-up fashion of a generation later.

The storming of the Bastille in 1789 marked the beginning of the French Revolution, and from this time onwards all the influences we have been considering speeded up a dramatic change in the clothes both of men and women. All privilege and all artificiality were to be swept away; there was to be a real return to nature. Now, as we have already noted, in the case of men this meant adopting English country clothes instead of French Court costume. In the case of women it meant something much more drastic. Obviously, a return to nature, in its literal sense, was an impossibility. It would have meant a return

4

75

Lady in Walking Dress. *Engraving by C. Grignion after H. Gravelot, 1744.*

Two Ladies at Ranelagh. *Engraving,
1775.*

Mrs Abington. *Engraving by J. Taylor,
1777.*

76

to the fur garments of the caveman, or even to complete nudity. The men who had made the French Revolution did not look quite so far back for their models. Instead they turned to the days of Ancient Greece and Rome. And, once the first revolutionary fervour was over, and fashionable clothes became possible again, women's clothes at least showed a marked tendency to copy those of classical times. The lines of dresses were vertical like those of Greek draperies and entirely white, because, although many ancient statues were originally polychrome, those that have come down to us and are to be found in museums are white.

Women's dresses in the 1790s therefore showed a complete break with tradition. They showed quite plainly that there had been a great social upheaval, for it does seem that in post-crisis periods women's clothes tend to be straight in line, pale in colour and with the waist in the wrong place. Something very similar is to be seen in dresses after the First World War. Post-crisis dresses are always 'little girl' dresses, for it is in such periods that the young woman attains a degree of emancipation and, so to speak, calls the tune. The fact that the waist is in the wrong place (very high in the period following the French Revolution, and very low in the period following the First World War) is symbolic of the fact that post-crisis periods are never strait-laced, either physically or morally.

Older people, were, of course, horrified. The dresses of the mid-1790s seemed to them to be little better than nudity. Instead of the elaborate paniers and stomachers of former ages, women, especially young women, wore a single garment of diaphanous material. Dresses were split up the sides, to the knee and beyond, and revealed limbs clothed in flesh-coloured tights or sometimes not clothed at all. The bodice was cut very low. On the feet were flat-heeled slippers, sometimes cross-gartered up the leg. In contrast with the elaborate *coiffures* of the *Ancien Régime* hair was worn short. It is a strange commentary on the frivolity of the period that, since the victims of the Revolution had had their hair cut short before they were executed, the new style was known as *à la victime*. Some French-women even went so far as to have a thin red ribbon tied round their necks to imitate the cut of the knife.

The fashionable young women of the time were known as *Merveilleuses*. Their male counterparts were known as *Incroyables* and the costume they wore was a curious blend of fashionable fantasy and English country clothes. The *Incroyable* was in fact a kind of caricature of the English country gentleman. His clothes were made of lighter materials in more violent colours. There were stripes everywhere, extending even to the stockings. The tails of the riding coat were incredibly elongated so that they almost touched the ground, the waistcoats so diminished that they scarcely covered the chest, and the neck-cloth so exaggerated that it concealed the chin and made all men look as if they were suffering from goitre. The hair was unpowdered and wildly dishevelled, and the hat was neither the tricorn of the previous age nor the top-hat of the future, but a kind of crescent moon, sometimes of huge dimensions. English people, however, never adopted the extravagant modes prevalent on the other side of the Channel. There had been no revolution in England. What happened here was merely that younger men began to wear in town the clothes which had formerly been thought suitable only for the country: the plain cut-away coat, top-boots, stout leather breeches and the high-crowned narrow-brimmed hat originally designed as a kind of crash-helmet in the hunting field. Coats had now been provided

A Spencer and a Threadpaper. *Caricature, 1792.*

78

with collars and lapels, but the skill of tailors was not yet sufficient to make the collars lie down on the shoulders, and they therefore tended to stick up vertically at the back of the neck. The waistcoat sometimes had a stand-up collar also and under it was often worn another waistcoat, the visible portion of which might be of some bright colour. A striking innovation was the use of gallowses or braces, made necessary by the fact that breeches came very much higher up the body than they had done earlier in the century and needed something of the kind to keep them in place. The usual materials for breeches were buckskin, linen or cashmere.

In 1795 the British Government imposed a tax on hair-powder, and this led to the general abandonment of wigs except among the men of learned professions. Opponents of the Government began to wear their own hair short, sometimes brushed forward over the forehead in a dishevelled manner.

In spite of the political differences between the two countries Frenchmen continued to suffer from Anglomania, and Englishwomen continued to draw the inspiration for their dresses from Paris. The latter process was much facilitated by the invention of the fashion-plate. It is true that this was not entirely a new invention for, as early as 1778, print sellers in Paris had conceived the idea of issuing coloured prints of the prevailing male and female fashions of the day. Before this, fashion news had been supplied to outlying places like England through the medium of little dolls, dressed in the latest Parisian modes and exported for purposes of copying. Marie-Antoinette's dressmaker, Rose Bertin, made a yearly tour of Europe with a coach-load of such little dolls; but this was at best a somewhat clumsy method of procedure. Fashion-plates could be much more easily transported. The publication known as *La Gallérie des Modes*, in spite of the fact that it appeared at irregular intervals, was a real fashion magazine. It consisted of a magnificent series of coloured plates, all very carefully described, and lasted from 1778 until 1787. After this was a gap until 1794 when a Swiss artist named Nicolaus von Heideloff began to publish, in London, the *Gallery of Fashion*. This publication was issued in monthly parts, each containing two coloured prints, and it lasted for exactly nine years. The total number of prints issued by Heideloff was therefore more than 200 and they provide a spendid panorama of the clothes worn during the last decade of the eighteenth century. An interesting point is the variety of dresses felt to be necessary for the fashionable woman. There are walking dresses, riding dresses, seaside dresses (a new thing this, for until the last quarter of the eighteenth century, no one had thought of going for a holiday to the seaside), evening dresses and Court dresses. The last looked very odd for hoops were still worn at Court and the attempt to combine them with the new fashionable line resulted in some very odd garments indeed. Between the evening dresses and the day dresses there is less difference than might be expected for both were long, sometimes with a train, both had low necks and both were, in general, white. From 1794 to 1797 there was a fashion for wearing two or three enormous ostrich plumes in the hair and these persisted, curiously enough, in Court dress into our own day.

The scantiness of dresses led to the popularity of large fur muffs and to the introduction of wraps, cashmere shawls, or sometimes mere handkerchiefs disposed like fichus to protect the throat. The flimsiness of the materials of which dresses were made and the absence

80

Ladies in Walking Dress. *Etching by N. Heideloff, 1794.*

of an under-petticoat made it impossible to insert pockets in the garments themselves and this led to the invention of the reticule or handbag. It was much laughed at but has survived several periods of eclipse to become, in our own day, the most necessary accessory of female costume.

Walking Dress. *Fashion Plate, 1807.*

CHAPTER EIGHT

The Nineteenth Century
I 1800-1850

When the nineteenth century opens we find that the real revolution which had taken place in male attire has been generally accepted. Apart from military and naval uniforms and ceremonial dresses, the male costume consisted of top-hat, cut-away coat, breeches and riding boots. The breeches did not end at the knee like those of the eighteenth century but ran down into the boots, and these might either be Hessians (a half-boot with a little tassel in the front) or boots with turn-over tops like those worn by modern jockeys. Knee breeches were still good form in the evening, but it was possible to wear tight-fitting pantaloons instead. Trousers were still only worn by sailors, children and the lower classes. In order to make them as tight-fitting as possible, breeches were sometimes made of elastic fabric such as stockinet. A popular material was buff or yellow nankeen imported from China.

Perhaps the most striking thing about male costume at this period was its sombre hue: dark blue, green and brown being the usual colours. The day of the embroidered coat was over and it was no longer possible to indicate social superiority by a display of gold lace. A duke could no longer be distinguished by the orders on his coat. 'All gentlemen are equal', might have been the motto of George Brummell, known as Beau Brummell, acknowledged by all his contemporaries to be the King of the Dandies. The well dressed man, thought Brummell, should never be conspicuous by his clothes; he should wear no strong colours, no patterning of any kind. Only one kind of superiority was possible: superiority of fit.

When we examine some of the actual garments which have come down to us from the eighteenth century we are compelled to realize how very badly they were made. The eighteenth century coat, especially of the embroidered variety, never fitted in the modern sense at all. It was a long time before tailors became sufficiently skilful to give a coat *revers*

83

or a collar. Such things needed considerable skill in cutting and the English tailors, who had been for some years accustomed to deal with a much heavier kind of cloth than their French counterparts, were much more skilful. By the opening years of the nineteenth century English tailors had established the pre-eminence which they have held ever since. Brummell himself was so particular about fit that he had his coat made by one tailor, his breeches by another and his waistcoat by a third. He was so particular about the fit of his neck-cloth that he is said to have discarded a dozen failures every morning before he was satisfied. He was a fanatic for clean linen, and very fastidious about the polish of his boots. There have been fine clothes before in history, but the word dandy was an English word and dandyism was an essentially English thing, the cult of which extended far beyond the country of its origin. So far as men's clothes are concerned the nineteenth century belongs to the English.

When we think of a nineteenth century man we think of him as wearing trousers, but these only gradually made their way into formal attire. Indeed it is recorded that the great Wellington himself was once refused admission to Almack's, the fashionable dance room of the period, on the grounds that he was improperly dressed—that is, that he was wearing trousers. However the (rather premature) victory parades held in London in 1814 gave trousers a new impetus. They were worn, in rather a voluminous form with a tie-string round the ankles, by the Cossack horsemen who created so much admiration when they paraded through the streets. After the Battle of Waterloo trousers began to be increasingly worn, especially in summer, when they were usually of white duck. By 1820 they had established themselves in general use. In evening dress, however, knee breeches or tight-fitting pantaloons continued to be worn for another decade or more.

A notable feature of male attire at this period was the greatcoat or overcoat often with multiple capes. There was also a curious overcoat called a spencer. This was a short coat without tails and was thought to have derived its name from the eccentric Earl Spencer who, having burnt the tails of his coat whilst standing in front of a blazing fire, instructed his tailor to cut them off and appeared in the street without them.

The top-hat was now universal and could take various forms. The brim was always narrow, but the high crown could have vertical sides, gradually narrowing upwards or slightly widening towards the top. This last style first appeared about 1819 and became the recognized fashionable form during the next decade. A crescent-shaped cocked hat was still in use in the evening as it could be crushed flat and carried under the arm. The material used for men's hats was felt or beaver. The hair was worn short but many of the younger men were no longer clean-shaven as almost all men had been during the previous century. Moustaches were only worn by cavalry officers but side whiskers became quite common.

We have noted the success of the English tailors in imposing their mode upon the whole of Western Europe. In women's dress it was the French who triumphed, with one curious interlude which has been generally ignored by historians of fashions. Between the Peace of Amiens in 1802 and the first abdication of Napoleon in 1814, England and France were engaged in desperate hostilities and Englishwomen were for a time cut off from news of the latest Paris modes. Englishwomen's fashions therefore developed along lines of their own. The waist slipped back into its normal place and the bodices were provided with

85

Evening Dress. *Fashion Plate, 1810.*

French and English Costume, 1814. *From* Le Bon Genre.

little slashed sleeves supposed to resemble those of the Elizabethans and Jacobean epochs. When Englishwomen rushed over to Paris in 1814 they found the French modes had developed quite differently. The French had retained the high waists but the skirts no longer fell loosely to the ankle. They were slightly shorter and had begun to spread out at the hem and to be decorated with frills or ruching. The corsage was no longer cut low in the daytime and round the neck was worn a collar slightly resembling those of the Elizabethans. Englishwomen immediately adopted the French modes with enthusiasm and for the rest of the century the dominance of Paris was unquestioned, so far as female costume was concerned.

A real change came in 1820, when the waist once more resumed its normal place. We have noted that a waist in the wrong place (either very high as in the years following the French Revolution or very low as in the years following the First World War) is a sign of social upheaval and an abandonment of accepted standards of conduct. Conversely, the return of the waist to its normal position is a sign that the post-crisis period is over. When the French aristocrats returned from exile in 1815 many no doubt imagined that they would be able to put the clock back to the days of the *Ancien Régime*; but too much water— and blood—had flowed under the bridges for this to be possible. There were to be no more powdered heads and embroidered coats. What the Restoration of the French monarchy did, however, was to inaugurate a new period of prudery as a reaction against the licence of the previous age. Prudery always manages to manifest itself most clearly in women's clothes and soon we find no more semi-transparent gowns and low-cut bodices. Dresses rose to the throat and were finished with a frill of lace; even evening dresses became slightly higher than they had been, and ladies began to make up for the shortness of their sleeves by wearing long white gloves, a custom which persisted well into the twentieth century. An increasing number of petticoats began to be worn and this was another factor in the return to a normal waist. To wear many petticoats with a high waist is to create a figure which bulges out immediately below the armpits, with very ungraceful results. When the waist is in its natural position, the effect of wide skirts is to make it look even narrower than in fact it is, and a slim waist was soon looked upon as desirable for its own sake. Corsets therefore came back again and tight lacing began again in earnest.

Apart from tight lacing and voluminous skirts there is another way of making waists look small and that is by exaggerating the size of sleeves. Sleeves played such an important part in the development of fashion in the 1820s and 30s that they were worth considering in some detail. The Restoration was itself an attempt to return to the past, but it was only part of the larger movement known as Romanticism. This was to be observed all over Europe. In England Sir Walter Scott was turning men's thoughts to the Medieval and Renaissance periods. In Germany Schiller's *Maria Stuart* had enormous influence even across the frontier in France. It is hardly too much to say that we cannot understand the dresses of the period unless we realize how completely Mary Queen of Scots dominated the thoughts of the dress designers in Western Europe in the ten years following the defeat of Napoleon. Everything was suddenly *à la Marie Stuart*. Every dress had to be furnished with a ruff and every sleeve had to be slashed in a not very successful attempt to imitate the modes of the mid-sixteenth century. In 1820 such sleeves were still quite small but the tendency of the time, was, as we have noted, to make sleeves larger and in the late 20s it became the custom to cover the little puffed sleeve with another sleeve of net, much more voluminous. It was large at the shoulder in order to take in the puffed sleeve underneath, and sloped to the wrist in the shape of a leg of mutton. In the early 30s the transparent net sleeve was replaced by one of a more opaque material but of a similar shape and, once this shape had been established, it tended to grow ever larger and larger. The typical dress of the early 1830s had a full skirt (slightly shorter than it had been previously) and enormous balloon sleeves. The effect was completed by enormous hats adorned with plumes or ribbons. Large hats were worn even in the evening and at the theatre where they must have been a great nuisance to those sitting behind them. Older women preferred the turban—not the close-fitting turban of the early years of the century but a large floppy affair almost as big as the hats of the same period. The hats were made of straw, Leghorn being the most expensive, Dunstable straw slightly cheaper and rice straw cheaper still. In winter, hats were frequently covered with velvet and had linings of silk, satin or gauze. Gradually they became more like bonnets, with backward tilt and brims drawn down at the sides and held in position by ribbons tied under the chin. Hair was generally dressed smoothly from a centre parting but with rows of ringlets hiding the cheeks. Jewellery consisted of gold chains on which were hung little bottles of perfume and lockets. Mosaic and shell cameo brooches were fashionable, and there was a curious rage for coral ornaments in day wear. Shoes were still without heels but from 1827 onwards were square-toed. In the daytime it was fashionable for shoes and stockings to be of the same colour as the dress.

Towards the end of the 1830s there was a change in fashion, coinciding with the accession to the throne of the young Queen Victoria. This was in 1837, but fashion historians point out that the collapse of the balloon sleeve and the shrinking of the upper part of the costume is already to be noted in the middle of 1836. However that may be, by 1840, women's dress had assumed the forms which we think of as early Victorian.

A new idea of women had begun to emerge. Romanticism gave way to sentimentality and a demure passivity of mind and body. The flamboyant balloon sleeves had disappeared. The corsage fitted close to the body and was almost always lined and boned, with three bones placed fanwise in the centre and with side bones running up to the armpit. The sleeves were usually tight and a new device for fitting them in below the shoulder made it impossible to raise the arm beyond a right angle. Back fastenings of hooks and eyes made the services of a maid almost essential. Ladies were not supposed to do anything for themselves. In fact everything seems to have been done at this period to stress the dependence of women. Even in riding costume, where the upper part of the dress aped masculine modes, the skirts were so voluminous that it was almost impossible for a lady to dismount from her horse without the services of a groom. The skirts of all dresses were now very full and a new method of attaching the material to the waistband gave the effect of wider hips, an effect emphasized by the use of pads of horsehair or other material. Skirts reached almost to ground level, permitting an occasional glimpse of a small square-toed slipper.

Colours tended to be sombre, primary hues being considered vulgar; lilacs, myrtle

Scene in a Tavern, 1822. *From* Life in London.

Male and Female Costume. *Fashion Plate, 1837.*

Walking Dresses. *Fashion Plate, 1833.*

90

greens, lemon yellows and mushroom browns were the acceptable shades. Shawls of all kinds were extensively worn. In summer they could be made of *glacé* or figured silks, embroidered organdy, or fringed foulard, in winter of cashmere with woven or printed designs. Paisley shawls with their derivative Oriental patterns were very popular. Cloaks and mantles were really shawls with slight variations, such as armhole slits or loose sleeves.

Hats in the 1840s had almost completely disappeared. It is true that bonnets were worn, and these were no longer the bonnets of the 30s with brims standing well above and back from the face, but close-fitting 'coal-scuttles', the crown of the brim forming a horizontal line and the sides of the brim curved down over the ears. This reinforced the impression of modesty, it being impossible to see a woman's face from the side; and she herself could only look straight in front of her. The hair was drawn flat over the head from a central parting with ringlets covering the ears. These ringlets were worn somewhat longer in the evening—a fashion which sometimes necessitated the use of false hair. There was very little make-up, rouge being considered immodest, but a discreet use of pearl powder helped to give to the complexion what was known as an interesting pallor.

Men's dress at this period showed a similar evolution in the direction of sobriety, away from the flamboyant waistcoats, the watch chains and dangling seals, the padded coats and the pinched-in waists of the 1830s. The tail-coat with a rectangular cut-in was still worn both for evening and day dress, but in the evening it was usually black. Its place in the daytime was increasingly taken by the frock coat with skirts all the way round and reaching to two or three inches above the knee. The jacket, which had shorter skirts, was coming into fashion towards the end of the 40s and was mainly worn in the summer. The shirt in the daytime had ceased to be frilled and the collar was smaller although still up-right and kept in place by a cravat. This was usually black (white in the evening) and sufficiently ample to conceal the collar almost entirely. In informal dress a scarf neck-tie could be worn with no collar visible, and kept in place with a pin. This neck-cloth could be spotted or patterned in other ways and was popular with a type known as the sporting gent.

The top-hat was now universally worn in all ranks of society, from the duke to the dustman. In the early 40s it was very tall and cylindrical, but by the end of the decade was considerably smaller and tended to curve out very slightly towards the top. Low-crowned hats with wide brims called wideawakes were sometimes worn in the country. Hair was fairly short and most men now wore side whiskers, most of the face being clean-shaven. Moustaches at this period were very unusual.

Much thought has been given to the question of why men's clothes in the middle of the nineteenth century should have become so dark in colour and formal in line. It has been suggested that this was due in part at least to the dirtiness of the atmosphere in all great cities. In former ages the amount of coal consumed had not been sufficient to charge the air with impurities but now, for the first time in history, it was full of black smuts. A deeper reason perhaps, for fashion is never governed entirely by practical considerations, was the prevailing Puritanism. A new class had now risen to power, a middle class of factory owners and merchants, and although these men were not poor they still disliked display and extravagance. Puritans have always preferred black clothes, as can be seen quite plainly as far back as the seventeenth century. This impulse now took the shape of what was known as good form, and even the upper classes succumbed to it. There was now little or no difference between the dress of the prosperous manfacturer or merchant and the aristocrat. It was no longer thought permissible to proclaim your rank by a display of gold lace. The ideal of gentility had triumphed, and the example of the English Court under Victoria and Albert, and even of the French Court under Louis Philippe, was unlikely to challenge it.

An excellent notion of the prevailing opinion can be gathered from contemporary books of etiquette. The anonymous author of *The Habits of Good Society* published in the late 40s, after laying down the doctrine of simplicity and appropriateness, of never being conspicuous in any society, either by over- or under-dressing, gives details of the wardrobe of a well dressed man of the period. He must have, he says, four kinds of coats: a morning coat, a frock coat, a dress coat and an overcoat. The economically minded man might manage with four of the first (this seems a handsome allowance) and one of each of the others per annum. He then continues:

The dress of an English gentleman in the present day should not cost him more than a tenth part of his income on an average. Generally speaking a man with £400 a year should not devote more than £40 to his outward man. The seven coats in question should cost about £18, six pairs of morning and one of evening trousers will cost £9. Four morning waistcoats, one for evenings another £4. Gloves, linen, hats, scarves and neck-ties about £10, and the important item of boots, at least £5 more.

The well dressed man who employed a moderately priced tailor (and by modern standards the prices quoted seem extremely moderate) could therefore dress himself for under £50 a year.

The same author advised that the best walking dress for non-professional men was a suit of tweed of a uniform colour, ordinary boots, gloves—not too dark for the coat, a scarf with a pin in winter or a small tie of one colour in summer, a respectable black hat, and a cane. In London, where a man was supposed to make visits as well as to lounge in the Park, he recommends a coat of a very dark blue or black, or a black cloth cut-away, white waistcoat and lavender gloves. It was permitted to carry an umbrella, and if this was not done it was essential to carry a cane or walking stick. The gentleman, thus attired, could and did go anywhere in the world. Englishmen wore a black silk hat and a frock-coat of cloth even in tropical countries such as India: a strange instance of the conformity imposed by fashion.

Meanwhile women's skirts were spreading to even wider proportions, and by the middle of the decade they were becoming much more decorated, with horizontal lines of trimming or with flounces, sometimes scalloped. But very ample skirts heavily trimmed were becoming intolerable. A contemporary commentator tells us that 'in hot weather a lined silk dress with seven tucks in the skirt and five flounces is now a considerable burden'. The muslin summer dresses or flimsy ball dresses might be flounced, but for heavy material, lace, velvet and ribbons were recommended. One cannot help thinking that women's clothes of this period must have been excessively uncomfortable. The climate of England was presumably no colder than it had been in 1800 when women had been content to go

Walking Dresses. *Fashion Plate, 1840.*

Evening Dresses, 1848. *From* The Illustrated London News.

Walking Costume, c. 1785. *From the* Galerie des Modes.

Afternoon Dresses. *Fashion Plate, 1859.*

about in one flimsy wool or muslin garment. Now it was considered essential to wear a mass of clothes. A contemporary tells us: 'Flannels should always, during the day, in Summer as well as in Winter, be worn next to the skin over the whole body and arms down to the middle of the thighs.' The chemise was very large reaching to the knee and with a bottom hem four feet wide. Heavy petticoats were worn, the undermost being short and of some stiff material, such as horsehair. Over this was worn one or more flannel petticoats in winter, and above them two more petticoats—one plain one and one embroidered. The outermost petticoat was usually made of cambric, elaborately embroidered and trimmed with crotchet or lace. Over this was worn a camisole to protect the tight-fitting dress. With all this weight of clothes and tight lacing as well, it is not surprising that fainting fits were extremely common and that women who could afford it preferred to drive in victorias rather than to proceed on their own feet even for short distances. Working women of course had to manage as best they could. Most of them were in domestic service and they seem to have been almost as much encumbered by clothes as their mistresses.

Something must be said of the outdoor garments of this period. For women there was an immense variety of names—Casawecks, Varens, Polkas—but these were all merely variations of the same type of short jacket with loose sleeves made of cashmere or velvet and lined with silk. The *pardessus* was of three-quarter length, short to the waist and with sleeves long and hanging open. There were full length mantles and shorter mantlets, pelisses and cloaks. The so-called Russian mantle had a large pelerine cape and wide sleeves. Men's outdoor garments were almost equally various and even contemporary writers were baffled by their different names. There was the Chesterfield, which could be either double-breasted or single-breasted and reached down to mid-thigh. There was the paletot very similar in form to a frock-coat and there was the paletot-sac, a short unwaisted version of the same garment. There was the curricle coat with one or more capes, used when driving. There was the sleeved cloak, later to be known as an Inverness. Mackintoshes had been in use since the late 30s when a man of that name brought out his patent india-rubber cloth, but the garment was unpopular for some years owing to its offensive smell.

The 1840s were in many ways a turning point in European history. At the beginning of the decade railways had only just begun to be constructed; at the end they formed a network of easy communication over the whole of Europe. We have noted the sombreness of both male and female attire during these ten years and this is not altogether surprising for, so far as social conditions were concerned, it was not a happy epoch. Not without reason did people speak of the Hungry Forties. There was famine in Ireland and poverty everywhere. In the late 40s the slums of all great cities were stricken with cholera. It is not surprising that there was much unrest and the year 1848 has gone down to history as the Year of Revolutions. Thrones were toppling everywhere and even in stable England there was the alarming Chartist movement. It seemed for a moment as if revolutionary socialism would win the day. In fact, the middle classes triumphed and inaugurated a new period of prosperity and expansion.

96

Walking Dresses. *Fashion Plate, 1855.*

CHAPTER NINE

The Nineteenth Century
II 1850-1900

After the failure of the revolutionary movement in the late 40s, the clothes of the middle classes—the world of trade and finance—were influenced by two events: the Great Exhibition held in Hyde Park in 1851 and the return of a Napoleon to the throne of France. The man who had been elected as President of the Second Republic proclaimed himself Napoleon III and inaugurated the Second Empire. The Great Exhibition had only an indirect influence on fashion, but it was the first of the great World Fairs, and introduced many new machines for manufacture, new materials and new products. The advent of Napoleon III had a direct influence on fashion, for very soon after his accession the Emperor married beautiful Eugénie de Montijo and she and her husband determined to make their court the most fashionable in Europe.

This attempt was shortly aided by something quite new in the history of fashion: the rise of the male *couturier* or dressmaker. The pioneer, strangely enough, was an Englishman named Worth, who, having been an assistant in a London store, went to Paris in the 50s and created the first Fashion House—that is, an establishment which created fashion. Worth expected his customers to come to him; previously a dressmaker had been a woman who visited grand ladies' houses and received their instructions. Worth was the first great fashion dictator in so far as such a phrase has any meaning. His rise coincided with the triumph of the crinoline, and this is an event of such importance in the history of costume that it must be considered in some detail.

We have already seen in the last chapter that before the end of the 40s women's clothes had become so voluminous and heavy that they were a real burden on their wearers. We have already met the horsehair pad worn on the hips to make them look larger and the petticoat of horsehair intended to make the skirts stand out. The French word for horsehair is *crin* and the word crinoline was already used for a skirt-expanding device which

97

made use of horsehair; now, however, the term began to be given a very different application. It was essentially a revival of the hoops of the eighteenth century but much more scientifically and gracefully constructed. The new hoops were made of flexible steel, circular and of diminishing size like the ribs of an air-ship. These were sewn into an under-skirt, and it was then possible to give the impression of an enormous number of petticoats without, in fact, any petticoats being worn at all. The crinoline must have given its wearers a new sense of freedom, for underneath the great bell-shape of the outer skirts the limbs were free, no longer hampered by innumerable folds of cloth. The wearing of this garment however, required very careful management. It was necessary to walk with short, even steps, and there were complaints that English women, who tended to take longer strides than Frenchwomen, were unable to prevent the dress from riding up in front or the cage from wobbling as they walked. There was also considerable danger from fire. A flimsy dress stretched over a wide frame was extremely inflammable, and the newspapers of the period tell a melancholy tale of numerous young women burnt to death by their crinolines catching in the open fires of the period. Nevertheless it was impossible to be fashionably, or even decently, dressed without it. Every woman wore it, from fine ladies to domestic servants. A cartoon in *Punch* shows the lady of the house admonishing her cook because she was *not* wearing a crinoline: a garment one would have thought most unsuitable for the Victorian kitchen. Actresses wore it, even when they were impersonating characters of former ages. So prevalent was the fashion that in 1859 Sheffield was turning out enough crinoline frames for half a million crinolines a week.

COSTUME

Some of the dresses, even those worn in the daytime, were four to five yards in circumference round the hem. The Empress Eugénie is reputed to have worn a ball dress which contained 1,100 yards of tulle. The Empress had become the acknowledged leader of European fashion and her influence helped to confirm Paris as the originator of all new modes. Her own taste however was Spanish rather than French, and this is perhaps most noticeable in the abandonment of the dun shades of the 40s and the introduction of an increasing range of violent colours. We find day dresses of scarlet or of maroon embroidered with another colour such as blue. Emerald green and mauve were much worn. There was a passion for checks and even for tartans—one of the rare instances in which Queen Victoria may be said to have influenced the mode. Ball dresses were still usually white, especially for young women, but in 1864 we note a ball dress of magenta silk trimmed with strips of white tulle or tarlatan. Magenta (called after one of Napoleon III's victories in Italy) was the colour *par excellence* at the height of the popularity of the Second-Empire.

Skirts were long, but the swinging of the crinoline, especially in high wind, made it inevitable that not only the ankles but the legs should sometimes be seen. This would have been thought most improper in the 1840s, and now women took to wearing long white pantaloons edged with lace and reaching to below the knee. There was also a new interest in footwear. The heeled slippers were now only worn for dancing; for daywear both boots and shoes had heels, although these were seldom more than half an inch thick. The boots were short, ending just above the ankle and were usually made of such materials as cashmere with patent leather toes and heels. They could be laced up the inside or buttoned

98

Walking Dress Showing Crinoline, *c.* 1860.

Male Costume, 1864.

on the outer side, and sometimes had elastic sides. Stockings were now sometimes striped horizontally in black and red.

Hair at this period was dressed rather simply, being brought down smoothly from a centre parting and draped around the ears with a bun, or twisted round or plaited at the back of the head. Side ringlets were now out of fashion except for young girls. Many women wore a small cap in the house or in the evening. Out of doors the bonnet still reigned supreme, tied under the chin and forming a circular frame around the face. The trimming was usually inside and could consist of lace, tulle, ribbons and flowers. The bonnet became steadily smaller in size as the decade drew on. Hats began to make their appearance, but it was laid down that they were not to be worn on Sundays and never in church. Flexible straw hats were worn in the country, and in 1854 the round hat made its appearance. This was mushroom shaped and trimmed with ribbon round the crown with floating ends behind. Such hats were also called seaside hats.

Towards the end of the decade the so-called lounging jacket for men made its appearance and became more and more popular being looser and more comfortable than the frock coat or morning coat. A favourite form was the Tweedside originating in Scotland. It reached to mid-thigh and was unwaisted: a baggysack, as contemporaries called it. The colours were generally sombre but striped tartans and loud checks were sometimes worn in the country. The commonest form of neck-wear was a moderately broad neck-cloth tied in a flat bow at the front, but very narrow neck-ties were also used. The collar usually stuck up straight but was sometimes turned down over the neck-tie. There was considerable variety in overcoats, ranging from the long Chesterfield to the short pilot coat, with enormous buttons. There were also loose cape-like overcoats and cloaks. The Raglan cape was introduced in 1857. It was a loose garment with what we still call a Raglan sleeve, which was not fitted into a round armhole, but cut to a point running up into the collar seam. It was supposed to have been invented by Lord Raglan, the one-armed commander of the British Forces in the Crimea. It was often made of waterproof material.

There was beginning to be more variety in male head-gear. The top-hat was, of course, still necessary for all formal occasions, but wideawakes were also worn, and the second half of the decade saw the advent of the bowler, still known to us by the same name.

The crinoline reached its greatest dimensions in the early 60s, but about 1865 a change came over its form. It was no longer symmetrical, projecting as much to the front as to the back. Instead, it slipped backward, and the uppermost ring of steel became smaller; the dress seen from the side was like a right-angled triangle, the front of the skirt being represented by an almost upright line. In 1867 there was a new modification: the crinoline actually became smaller, and by the following year it was only half as wide as its wearer's height. Many ladies had begun to rely once more on petticoats alone, whilst some of the dresses were made with a mass of material bunched up behind in a kind of embryo bustle. Growing attention was now being paid to walking dresses, for the trailing crinoline skirts were very hampering in the street. One of the remedies, which originated in England and was later copied in Paris, was to have the lower edge of the skirt attached by strings to the waist in such a manner that it could be drawn up over the crinoline, exposing the lower edge of the underskirt and also, of course, the boots. This, though rather a daring fashion for the day, was also practical, and rapidly became popular. However, by 1868, in the words of a contemporary:

Day dresses may now be considered in two distinct classes; short skirts for morning wear, called *walking dresses* and dresses with long sweeping trains for carriage, flower shows, concerts and similar occasions, classified as *afternoon costumes*. Dresses are not now made long and caught up by loops for walking; a distinct class of dress is required for each occasion.

In other words a woman with any pretensions to elegance required several different *kinds* of dresses. Even day dresses however were so ample that they required some kind of support, though the general size was diminishing. A crinoline for a ball dress in the early 60s might have as many as thirty circular hoops. It must have been difficult to sit down in such a construction and in 1866 the crinoline was made to fold inwards when in a sitting position. In the same year appeared an undergarment known as the *peplum jupon*, a gored petticoat with three steels round the bottom, and a deep-pleated flounce. In the following year horsehair petticoats came into use once more. By 1869 the crinoline was hooped only at the back and in the same year appeared the crinolette or half-crinoline 'of steel half-hoops with horsehair or crinoline flounces forming a bustle'. The true crinoline which had dominated the fashions of the 50s and 60s was obviously coming to the end of its reign.

Women were also demonstrating their emancipation—a very small degree of emancipation by modern standards—by substituting hats for bonnets. Hats could assume many forms: wideawakes (imitated from those worn by men) with low crowns and wide limp brims, similar hats with low crowns and moderate stiff brims, small straw hats with crowns like flowerpots, and so-called Tyrolese hats of black silk or velvet which appeared about 1868. From about 1864 young women in particular took to wearing Glengarry Scotch caps and pork-pie hats. The latter were worn tilted forward over the forehead to make room for the heavy chignon which had now become fashionable. The chignon was nearly always large, and covered with a hairnet and for many women the use of false hair became a necessity; indeed the entire chignon was often false and was attached to the natural hair by means of a comb. Enormous quantities of false hair were imported from the remoter parts of Europe and even from China, to the great alarm to those who were concerned with public health.

With the 70s we seem to enter a new world of feminine fashion, in which the fundamental shape of the female figure is quite different from that of the previous two decades. In some strange way the crinoline had seemed to be the symbol of the French Second Empire, which came to a disastrous close in 1870. France was invaded and Paris besieged. As a centre of fashion the French capital was for the moment out of the running, and clothes became noticeably less extravagant. Many women began to make their dresses at home, and this was made much easier by the sewing machine, which had been perfected during the previous generation and was now comparatively cheap. One perhaps unfortunate development was the use of different materials for the same dress. It became usual to cut a dress out of two different materials, one patterned and one plain, and then to make one portion of the dress of plain material trimmed with the pattern, and the rest of the patterned

Evening Dresses. *Fashion Plate, 1868.*

104

Visiting Dresses. *Fashion Plate, 1874.*

material trimmed with the plain. The result was sometimes not unlike a patchwork quilt. Colours tended to be rather violent; we find dark red poplin trimmed with black velvet or green poplin trimmed with satin, although black continued to be popular for mantlets and similar garments worn out of doors. For summer there was a new fashion for striped foulards and sometimes tunics had striped and figured materials worn upon coloured silk dresses of a contrasting shade. Popular colours were metal green, bronze green and sulphur yellow.

A striking feature of the period was a dress composed of a separate bodice and skirt, and in 1877 the blouse—sometimes called the Russian blouse—made its appearance. In some ways the dresses of the 70s were even less practical than those of the 60s had been, if only because nearly all skirts had trains. This was a most unhygienic fashion, as a lady walking in the street inevitably brought back with her into the house dirt and dust collected from the pavement. Even a tennis-dress, for tennis was just beginning to make its way as a game for ladies, was furnished with a long train and, as the skirt was also very tight, any really vigorous action became impossible. Tight lacing was now as extreme as it had been in the 30s. Some ladies succeeding in reducing their waists to a circumference of nineteen inches.

About the year 1878 there was a new development, for the corset, for the first time since the eighteenth century, began to be worn over the skirt, and to form, as it were, part of the bodice, running down to a sharp point in front. The elaborate draperies of the skirt below it were intended to make the hips look larger, this being an obvious method of making the waist look smaller still. A contemporary notes: 'A well developed bust, a tapering waist and large hips are the combination of points recognised as a good figure.' The general effect, to the modern eye at least, was to make a woman look like a long, elaborately ribboned parcel; and it is not surprising that there were many people, especially artists and their friends, who began to hanker for a different kind of costume altogether.

The rebellion against fashionable modes was an essential part of what is known as the æsthetic movement. The æsthetic lady wore flat shoes, no corsets, and a loose robe with wide sleeves, vaguely derived from dresses of the Renaissance period. Sometimes her dress was embroidered or otherwise patterned with large sunflowers, the sunflower being the accepted emblem of the movement. Her male counterpart wore a costume consisting of knee breeches, loose flowing tie, braided jacket and a wideawake hat. Some æsthetic ladies adopted what they imagined was a version of Greek dress, but these so-called Greek dresses had far more in common with the contemporary mode than anything that was ever worn in ancient Hellas.

As a dress reform crusade, the æsthetic movement was a failure, but some of its principles, in particular its dislike of violently contrasting colours, had considerable influence on the fashions of the next decade.

The 1880s saw the appearance of what was known as the New Woman. Unlike her æsthetic sister, she was not artistic. She despised sunflowers and blue china, and went in for sport. Up to about the middle of the century the only sport open to ladies was riding. In the 60s came archery, a pastime which had little or no effect on costume as it could quite easily be practiced in an ordinary summer dress. In the 70s three new sports arose: roller-skating, making it possible to skate all the year round instead of only in winter (artificial ice-rinks had not yet been invented), croquet and lawn tennis. Tennis soon became extremely popular, less perhaps as a game than as a social occasion for bringing young people together, but it soon became obvious that it was very difficult to play in the encumbering feminine costume of the time. *Punch* in the late 70s even suggested that men should be handicapped while playing, by having scarves tied round their knees. A slightly more sensible costume was gradually evolved, although the complete emancipation of the female tennis player was not really arrived at until the 1930s.

A really important influence on women's clothes in the last quarter of the nineteenth century was due to the bicycle. So long as the bicycle was the penny-farthing with one large and one little wheel, it could not be ridden by women at all; but improvements in its construction were not long delayed and, about the year 1890, bicycling became a fashionable sport. In London fashionable ladies had their bicycles taken to Battersea Park by their servants on Sunday morning. They then went down in their carriages suitably attired for the sport, mounted their bicycles and rode solemnly round and round. But what should the costume of a lady cyclist be? It was obviously impossible for her to wear with comfort or even with safety the long trailing robes of the period. She was compelled to wear either a shorter or a divided skirt, or frankly to adopt the knickerbockers of the male cyclist. Some of the very voluminous knickerbockers of the period look very strange to modern eyes, but they represented a real revolution in feminine dress. Mrs. Bloomer had tried to introduce in the early 50s a divided garment for women. She met with little but ridicule, until the bicycling age began and women wore breeches at last.

The new enthusiasm for sport had considerable influence on male costume also. As early as the 60s knickerbockers had been adopted for shooting and also for croquet. Football was at first played in knickerbockers or in short trousers just covering the knee. Cricket continued to be played in long trousers as it is played today. In the 70s appeared skating costumes for men consisting of long trousers and short jackets edged with fur or astrakan. The new enthusiasm for yachting brought in monkey jackets, pilot coats and reefers of blue serge. Throughout the 80s the Norfolk jacket was gradually increasing in popularity, being worn in the country with knickerbockers, and a bowler or deer-stalker hat.

During the 90s it became possible to classify men's clothes more clearly as formal or informal wear. In the West End of London at 11 o'clock in the morning, it was still impossible for a gentleman to be seen in anything but a shiny top-hat and a frock-coat or morning coat. The frock-coat had silk lapels and was worn with a waistcoat which could be either white or grey, striped trousers and stiff white collar. It was now more frequently seen than a morning coat cut away in front; but the lounge suit, derived from the sporting clothes of a previous generation, was becoming more common, not only in the country, but for informal occasions in town. The strange thing is that a stiff white collar was worn with this outfit as it was with more formal dress. In the evening it was more usual to wear what we call full evening dress: that is, a tailed coat; but for dining at home or at a club, more and more men were adopting the dinner-jacket which had first appeared in the early 80s. A stiff white shirt was worn with both.

Women's clothes in the last twenty years of the nineteenth century went through some

Male Costume, Formal and Informal. *Fashion Plate, 1881.*

Cycling Costume, 1895.

Ball Dress, 1895.

surprising evolutions. The small-hipped fashion of 1880 was replaced in the middle of the decade by a new bustle, not the mere bunching up of the clothes behind which had been fashionable in the 70s, but a kind of vertical shelf sticking out from the back. This was kept in place by an extraordinary contraption of wire netting and sometimes of steel springs. By 1890 this too had vanished and skirts were once more smooth over the hips, but, unlike the skirts of 1880, they flared out widely at the hem. They were cut on the bias to make them fit more closely, and tight lacing was extreme. This remained the mode for the whole of the decade; indeed the only way in which fashion shows any important modification between 1890 and 1900 is in the matter of sleeves. At the end of the 1880s the sleeve was set in the bodice in such a way as to produce a slightly gathered effect, a little peak of material at each shoulder. At first such sleeves were tight, but they soon showed signs of expanding, and by 1893 a leg-of-mutton effect was seen. Soon the sleeves were so large that cushions were necessary in order to keep them in place. They reached their largest dimensions in 1895, and are depicted in their most extravagant form in the posters of Toulouse-Lautrec.

A new development was the tailor-made coat and skirt. This was essentially an English fashion but was not without its influence on the modes of Paris. The blouse was very popular as it could be worn with any skirt and either bought ready-made or run up at home Blouses, however, were sometimes very elaborate, with cascades of lace down the front; evening blouses were popular in the middle of the decade. Evening dresses in general had a deep square or V-shaped *décolletage* sometimes with shoulder straps and no sleeves. With this was worn the short mantle with its high Medici collar so characteristic of the period.

Head-gear and methods of dressing the hair showed considerable variety during this

110

Walking Dress, 1899.

period. In 1880 the hair was worn in a little coil at the back of the head, and with a fringe over the forehead. The small hats were worn rigidly upright, sometimes with feathers to increase the apparent height. The middle of the 80s shows extremely small hats perched on the top of the head, and two years later the very sharp-pointed hats, high and narrow, echoed the general lines of the dress. Hats varied during the next few years in the most extraordinary fashion, being wider in 1889, 1891 and 1893, and smaller in 1890 and 1892. There was a temporary fashion for wearing men's hats: either a smaller version of the homburg or the straw boater perched forward over the forehead.

The last decade of the nineteenth century was, in a very real sense, a period of transition. Young people at least were beginning to grow tired of what was regarded as the stuffiness of the Victorian Age. The New Woman was struggling to be free, and yet was unwilling to relinquish the advantages of dependency. The dresses of the period suggest an odd blend of freedom and restraint, and this mental conflict, according to the fashion historian Dr. Willett Cunnington, 'found expression in a taste for discordant colours; yellow trimmed with pink and green; violently contrasting in material and colour with the rest of the gown. A pink skirt and a black bodice. Often bodice and skirt seemed hardly on speaking terms.' The favourite colour of the decade was undoubtedly yellow, and it is perhaps symbolic that the magazine which was creating most stir among advanced people was the *Yellow Book*. New movements were everywhere in the ascendant. In manners, morals and everything else, the nineteenth century was clearly drawing to a close.

Ski-ing Costume, 1906.

112

CHAPTER TEN

The Twentieth Century

The death of Queen Victoria early in the new century seemed to symbolize the end of an epoch. The new Monarch was reputed to be fond of pleasure and what was known as high life, and the Edwardian period is usually thought of as an age of gaiety and extravagance. From the point of view of fashion it had two very striking characteristics. One was the new invention of the flared skirt which, unlike any previous skirt, was neither straight nor convex, but concave. It was, in fact, bell-shaped. It was fitted closer over the hips by the aid of tucks or pleats, and it looked best when worn by a tall woman. The other element was the so-called health corset, a corset boned in such a way as to throw the hips back and the bosom forward. This too favoured the tall and mature type of woman, and gave her the peculiar stance so characteristic of the period. The S-shaped look was further accentuated by the Russian blouse and the cascades of lace descending from the bust. Never since the seventeenth century had so much lace been worn but of course it was now only worn by women. There were lace collars and collarettes, lace sleeves, lace plastrons, lace over-bodices, and lace petticoats only to be glimpsed occasionally but requiring the finest workmanship. Real lace in such quantities being unobtainable and machine-made lace somewhat despised, a compromise was discovered in Irish crotchet for which there was a considerable vogue. The hair was built high on the head, and the flat pancake hats projected forward as if to balance the trailing skirts. Evening dresses were often deeply _décolleté_ in front, but day dresses concealed everything of the body except the face and hands, and even the latter were often hidden by gloves. The neck was entirely encased in a _jabot_ or collar of lace reaching almost to the tips of the ears, and often kept in position by little boned supports. It seemed to be thought essential that the human neck should be completely concealed, for men's collars—even on country clothes and cycling outfits—consisted of perpendicular cylinders of stiff linen, and for their tailor-made and country clothes women also adopted these masculine collars.

113

In some matters there was a slight departure from formality. The frock-coat and top-hat were still considered essential on all formal occasions, but for ordinary wear the lounge suit and homburg hat had by this time established themselves. The skirts of the coat, however, were considerably longer than those of today, and the coat itself was split up the back. In summer a straw hat of the circular boater variety was much worn; it was even sometimes worn with riding breeches. A lounge suit with matching coat and trousers was often worn with a waistcoat of different material, coloured in winter and white in summer. The trousers were extremely narrow, and many young men were beginning to wear them with permanent turn-ups. The trouser-press, which had been invented in the middle 1890s, gave them the sharp edges which are still popular today.

A striking innovation in this period was the increased popularity of tailor-made clothes for women. Women were beginning to engage in many occupations which would have been thought impossible in the Victorian era, and governesses, typists and shop assistants were choosing to wear plain and workmanlike costumes very different from the garden party dress of the idle rich. Even rich women wore tailor-mades in the country or for travelling, and since the prestige of English tailors was the highest in the world, the domination of Paris as a centre of fashion was seriously challenged at this epoch.

A certain modification in the general outline of dress was to be seen in the year 1908. The exaggerated overlap of the blouse was abandoned, and the bust was no longer thrust quite so far forward as before. Skirts became a little narrower at the hem, although they still trailed on the ground, and required to be gathered up in the hand when crossing a wet or muddy street. The high waisted Empire gown tended to make tight lacing less extreme. By 1910 these tendencies had resulted in a new style. The S-shape was entirely abandoned and women resumed their upright position. The top of the corset was lower, leaving the bosom free, but it now strove to diminish the apparent size of the hips. The skirts, instead of being flared out at the hem, were narrow, sometimes so narrow that they made it difficult for women to walk. This tendency culminated in the hobble-skirt of 1911 which was worn with an immensely wide hat. There was however another influence which had a marked effect at this period. All fashionable clothes began to take on a curious Oriental look, as if Western women (in spite of the current activities of the Suffragettes) had suddenly decided to adopt the costume of the harem. This Orientalism was due to the Russian ballet, and in particular to Léon Bakst's designs for *Shéhérazade*, and to Paul Poiret, the leading Parisian designer of the time. There was a new rage for violent colours, the colours of Edwardian dresses having favoured pastel shades. So powerful was the Oriental impulse that some bold women even began to wear what was called the harem-skirt, with little baggy trousers visible beneath its hem. This fashion, however, produced an astonishing amount of hostility and women wearing the harem-skirt were chased off the streets. The hobble-skirt however was universally worn, impractical as it was. The frilly underskirt was entirely abandoned, as it was impossible to wear it with the new silhouette. In such narrow skirts it was also impossible to have pockets, and so the handbag or reticule returned. It was immensely large, like all the accessories of the period, including the fur muffs which were now extremely fashionable.

Early in 1912 there was another change in the silhouette. The straight effect of the

Ball Gown, 1903.

115

116

Fashion Plate, 1911.

skirt was modified by looping it up here and there, or by wearing over it a kind of tunic. Lace tunics were very fashionable even with day dresses. In evening dresses there was a craze for tunics of gold lace. By the end of 1913 the tunic effect with the draped skirt underneath might be described as the fundamental mode, and towards the middle of 1914 the so-called lampshade tunic had established itself, worn over a narrow and clinging underskirt.

There was a fundamental change in the neck-line. Instead of the high collars of the previous decade there came in what was known as the V-neck, in spite of the opposition of the clergy, who denounced it as immoral, and many of the doctors, who denounced it as dangerous to health. As a matter of fact we should consider the V-necks of 1914 to be extremely modest.

The outbreak of war in 1914 had very little immediate effect on feminine fashion. There was no striking and sudden abandonment of an old costume, and change, when it did come, came gradually. Skirts remained long and rather narrow with, over them, a kind of flared out-tunic about knee-length, but the long narrow skirt underneath was soon found to be an encumbrance in all the new occupations which were now open to women after the disappearance of the men into the armed forces. By a happy inspiration the underskirt was abolished altogether and the tunic slightly lengthened, so that, by the middle of 1915, feminine dress had assumed the essential form which it was to keep throughout the whole period of the War. With short skirts in the daytime were worn little boots reaching almost to the bottom of the skirt, and these shortish skirts and high-laced boots lasted with little modification until the end of the War.

Even before 1914 there had been a considerable reduction in the size of hats, and hair began to be dressed much closer to the head. Hats were adorned with feathers, projecting at all kinds of odd angles. It was considered chic to have two feathers pointing in opposite directions, and this is the characteristic head-dress of the first two years of the conflict. In 1917 most women dressed their hair with a coil at the back, worn rather high just behind the crown; but those engaged in war work had already found the convenience of short hair, although it was by no means so short as it was afterwards to become. There were many long bobs rather like those of the fifteenth century page. The hat in most general use was a kind of large billy-cock, fitting closely to the head, the ancestor of the later cloche.

Evening dresses, owing to war conditions, suffered something of an eclipse. They were in general rather high-waisted, and there was a vogue for a semi-transparent tunic There was a marked decline of *décolletage*, and many women adopted the compromise of the house-frock, which could be worn from tea-time onwards. It was the equivalent of the modern cocktail dress, cocktail parties being, of course, still in the future. Fur was a very favourite trimming for both day and evening dresses. Blouses were much worn, and as knitting had now become one of the main occupations of women not actively engaged in war work, there was a vogue for the jumper made to slip over the head without fastenings. In 1918 there was an attempt to introduce a National Standard Dress, a utility frock, without hooks or eyes or metal buckles and designed to serve as 'outdoor gown, house gown, rest gown, tea gown, dinner gown, evening dress and nightgown'. In 1919 the flared skirt was replaced by the so-called barrel line. This attempt to make women look tubular would have been marred by any protrusion of the bosom and so we find for the first time in history an attempt to flatten it, and even to deny its existence altogether. All these tendencies pointed forward to the schoolboy shape fashionable between 1919 and 1924.

It was as if women were striving to look as much like boys as possible. A small bust and small hips were admired, and the age-long attempt to give the impression of a slim waist was abandoned altogether. The corset therefore became unnecessary. It was given up completely or shrank to a mere belt from which the stockings could be suspended. Once the pretence of having a waist had been abandoned there was no reason why the waist-line should remain in its normal position. Instead of rising as it had done immediately after the French Revolution it showed a tendency to sink, and already in 1923 was round the hips. It was to remain there until the end of the decade. The modes which resulted have been described as 'little girl' fashions and this was natural enough, for during the war it was the very young woman who had found economic independence and so was able to call the tune. The skirt however remained long, and it was not until 1925 that, for the first time in history—civilized history at least—women began to expose their legs.

This was a startling revolution, and older people were extremely shocked by it. Perhaps every age is shocked by the way in which the young behave, but in the 20s it really seemed as if young women were deliberately breaking away from all the restraints which had been imposed upon them in former times. The leaders of the rout were known as the Bright Young Things, and their doings filled the columns of the daily papers. They drank cocktails—deadly American mixtures of which the British public were now learning for the first time. They painted their faces, and had no hesitation about doing it in public. The use of the bright scarlet lipstick became universal. Most shocking of all, perhaps, they cut off their hair. The bob gave way to the shingle and that in turn to the Eton crop. Short hair was indeed imperative if one was to wear the now universal cloche hat.

Another striking innovation of the period was the appearance of flesh-coloured silk or artificial silk stockings. Before 1924 black and other dark coloured stockings had been usual, but now it was only the seam up the back which showed whether a girl was wearing stockings or not. The new mode had at least the effect of emphasizing the need to pay very much more attention to and to spend much more money on stockings and shoes than had ever been done before. Stockings became an important item in the working girl's budget and although a new method of producing them inexpensively had been discovered, they were not really cheap if one took into consideration the very small amount of wear which they gave. An attempt to protect them by wearing what was known as the Russian boot never spread to fashionable circles. If the makers of silk stockings were enjoying a boom, manufacturers of dress materials were beginning to complain that so little stuff was used in the ordinary dress, that their sales were seriously affected. Dressmakers also saw their business menaced as the extreme simplicity of the prevailing mode made it easier for women to make their clothes at home.

Meanwhile men's clothes were showing a stready progress away from formality. The frock-coat disappeared altogether, and the morning coat and silk hat were only worn on ceremonial occasions. The lounge suit was now universal, worn with a soft collar and a homburg hat. In the country men wore sports jackets and flannel trousers. The especially

119

Evening Dresses, 1919.

Day Dresses, 1928.

120

Evening Dress, 1929.

wide trousers known as Oxford bags came in in 1924 and trousers remained wide until the end of the 1930s. For golf and other sports, men wore the baggy knickerbockers known as plus-fours, often with a gaily coloured Fair Isle sweater.

In feminine fashion the extreme of short skirts and short hair was reached in 1927. It was now impossible for a woman to sit down without showing her knees; for day wear this short skirt lasted until 1930. Evening modes, however, had already, by careful degrees—tails, trains, side-pieces and transparent hems—become long again, and in 1930 day skirts suddenly lengthened to mid-calf or lower and the waist slipped back into its normal position. The universal cloche was abandoned in favour of an immense variety of hats; the only rule was that they had to be extremely small and poked forward over one eye. There was a temporary vogue for large sleeves, not as in 1830 and 1895 to decrease the apparent size of the waist, but to make the hips look smaller. The emphasis throughout the 1930s was on slim hips and backless dresses, and sometimes the whole outfit looked as if it had been designed to be seen from the back. The shoulders were heavily padded to make them look square and wide. This was a very curious fashion. Perhaps never before in the whole history of dress had it been considered a beauty in a woman to have shoulders wider than her hips. The idea was to look like Greta Garbo, and it is an interesting question as to how far the popularity of this Scandinavian star was responsible for the fashion, and how far her own prestige was dependent upon it.

Throughout the 30s there was a marked decrease in the difference between the clothes of wealthy women and those less well-off. Most women in all classes were now engaged in some kind of gainful occupation and they tended to wear a kind of working uniform consisting of that essentially English costume, the tailor-made. Trousers, in the form of slacks, were increasingly worn for sport, but not yet for shopping. There was a marked division between day clothes and evening clothes; for even girls belonging to the lower income groups (factory workers and the like) wore some kind of evening dress—often based on something they had seen in the cinema. This tended to stabilize fashion, for most films are shot at least two years before they are generally released. The evening dresses of the 30s were therefore curiously static, and looked rather like fancy dress.

During the decade there was a marked development in sports clothes. Tennis dresses at the end of the 20s had been very similar in length and general outline to ordinary wear; but when skirts went long again in 1930 tennis players were naturally reluctant to follow suit. Skirts worn for tennis therefore remained short and began to look like a specialized sports costume. Then in 1931 Mrs. Fearnley-Whittingstall, playing at Forest Hills in the United States of America, appeared on the court with bare legs. In spite of some opposition the stockingless mode triumphed. In the same year Señorita de Alvares played in divided skirts which came to slightly below the knee, and two years later Miss Alice Marble of San Francisco appeared in shorts above the knee. This has now become the recognized tennis costume for women all over the world.

There were striking alterations in the design of bathing costumes during this period. In the 20s bathing costumes had been almost as ample as day dresses but they gradually became shorter and shorter, and in 1930 appeared the first backless bathing costume—no more backless, however, than the evening dresses of the period. It was not bathing itself

Walking Costume, 1937.

Plus Fours, 1935.

but the new enthusiasm for sun-bathing which was really responsible for this mode.

In 1939 the skirts of day dresses suddenly became shorter again, reaching to just below the knee. Evening dresses, however, remained long and some were even provided with a revived crinoline. With it came the first suggestion of a return to tight lacing. Both in Paris and in London the dress designers seemed determined to bring in tight waists, and they might have succeeded if there had been no war. Even the actual declaration of war seemed to make very little difference as was seen in March 1940 when all the great Paris houses launched their collections, apparently oblivious of the fact that France was on the eve of the greatest defeat in its history. After the fall of Paris England was as completely cut off from French fashions as she had been in the Napoleonic wars. Indeed, once clothes rationing had been introduced in June 1941, fashion in England may be said to have ceased to exist. Women were compelled to wear any clothes that they could get. House-wives as well as factory workers took to wearing slacks, thereby making stockings un-necessary, and even with skirts some women began to go about with bare legs. Many women painted their legs and drew a line down the back to imitate the seam. Hats were replaced by head-scarves and in wet weather by plastic hoods. Even when communication with France was restored in 1945 there was very little change, for clothes rationing was made even more stringent than it had been during the war.

Then, in the spring of 1947, a young Paris designer called Christian Dior launched the New Look. This was quite different in form from anything that had been seen for a considerable number of years. The skirt was long, twelve inches or less from the ground, and wide at the hem. The shoulders were narrow and rounded and there were little pads on the hips to make them look larger. This new dress provided a striking example of fashion's independence of economic considerations. Materials were in short supply, and in England, clothes rationing was still in force. The British authorities looked sourly at the new mode and did their best to discourage it; yet, within a year, it had won acceptance almost everywhere.

Students of fashion did not quite know what to make of it. The social upheaval of the Second World War might surely have been expected to have similar results to previous social upheavals such as those following the French Revolution and following the First World War. In both cases there had been a definite post-crisis dress: 'little girl' dresses, straight in line and with the waist in the wrong place—very high in 1800 and very low in 1925. One philosopher of fashion, however, was bold enough to prophesy that the New Look would not last very long and would inevitably be succeeded by a post-crisis fashion. He regarded the New Look as a back-eddy, a visible sign of women's unconscious desire to return to the conditions of a more settled age when servants were plentiful, and ladies led a sheltered life.

A curiously parallel movement could be observed in male costume, but here the reaction was not to Victorian but to Edwardian modes, with tighter trousers and jackets buttoned higher. There was even a revival of the bowler hat, worn just a size too small. This outfit became the recognized costume of upper class young men who were just, perhaps, de-mobilized from the Guards: these were the new Edwardians. But at the other end of the social scale were the Teddy Boys. They adopted the Edwardian modes but with some

The 'New Look', 1947.

significant variations, chiefly in the width of the shoulder. They were in consequence sometimes known as the 'wide boys'. They wore their hair long, and if they had a hat at all it was not the bowler but a soft felt hat strangely bashed in at the back. They wore vivid ties and their shirts were in lumber-jack checks. Between these two extremes there was a great variety in the clothes of the young, many of the items of which were derived from Army Surplus stores. The battle-dress blouse appeared on the golf course, and the motor cyclist found the sleeveless leather jacket a useful invention. Most influential of all was the duffle coat, a rough smock-like garment with a hood and rope and toggle fastenings of the kind worn by sailors in bad weather. All classes adopted this garment, and perhaps for the first time in history it was possible to see a man who prided himself on his appearance dressed in a town suit, a bowler hat and a duffle coat. Women also adopted the garment, sometimes wearing it with the new tapering pantaloons in some brilliant colour. This was something entirely new in the history of fashion.

Equally startling were some of the new bathing costumes. As we have noted, these had grown gradually less ample during the period between the wars, and in the 30s had been generally backless. Now there appeared a gap between the brassière, and the panties, and this gap grew ever wider until it reached its logical end in the bikini. Attempts were made by some of the authorities at seaside resorts to ban this garment, but, in the end, without effect. Sports clothes in general, especially for girls, became ever less ample, and young girl cyclists adopted what was almost a uniform—short-sleeved blouses and very short pants. For motor cycling, however, it was necessary to wear something warmer, and motor cyclists, both male and female, adopted something similar to flying kit with the very necessary addition of a crash helmet. With sports clothes, hats were not worn and even with town clothes many men began to go about, especially in summer, bare-headed. Women's hats were for the most part small and inconspicuous.

Evening dresses showed considerable variety. The skirts were, in general, long although skirts of ballet length were sometimes seen, and could be either straight in line or extremely *bouffant*, an effect which was obtained either by a crinoline or by wearing a petticoat of stiff nylon. Bodices were tight with a deep wide *décolletage*. Many dresses were strapless and were worn rather daringly low.

A slightly modified New Look persisted until the middle 50s when a new style was launched by the leading Paris designers. Once again Dior was one of the first in the field, with his A-look and, when this failed to catch on, his H-look. Both these modes, especially the latter, were a frank return to the fashions of the 20s so that those who had prophesied a typical post-crisis dress following the Second World War were justified. The tight waist was abandoned and lines of dresses were straight. The fashions of the last few years have shown little tendency to modify this essential line. But female fashion is never static and the one thing certain is that it will change again.

The future of men's clothes may perhaps be suggested with more confidence. For the last 200 years or more modification in men's attire has come by adopting a sports garment for ordinary wear, making it tighter and smarter in the process. This has happened over and over again, and there is little reason to suppose that it will not happen once more in the foreseeable future.

Index

127

Index

134